More to Life than More

More to Life than More

A Memoir of Misunderstanding, Loss, and Learning

ALAN PESKY & CLAUDIA AULUM

Skyhorse Publishing

Skyhorse Publishing books may be purchased in bulk at special discounts for sales promotion, corporate gifts, fund-raising, or educational purposes. Special editions can also be created to specifications. For details, contact the Special Sales Department, Skyhorse Publishing, 307 West 36th Street, 11th Floor, New York, NY 10018 or info@skyhorsepublishing.com.

Skyhorse® and Skyhorse Publishing® are registered trademarks of Skyhorse Publishing, Inc.®, a Delaware corporation.

Visit our website at www.skyhorsepublishing.com.

10 9 8 7 6 5 4 3 2 1

Library of Congress Cataloging-in-Publication Data is available on file.

Cover design by Heidi Worcester
Cover image by Wendy Pesky

ISBN: 978-1-5107-6635-8
Ebook ISBN: 978-1-5107-6659-4

Printed in the United States of America

```
          THERE'S MORE TO LIFE THAN MORE
                (for Alan)
Will it ever
   Be enough?
Will the next new car
   The stock market increase
      The shirt that will go next
         To all the other shirts
Will it ever be ██
   Enough?
      Will you live for the next
         To do list?
         Will you wake to check the next
            Paycheck?
      Or
            Will you maybe
               Perhaps
         Pause
            Maybe
               Perhaps
                  Breathe
      And know that you
         Have life
            And air
                  And love
         And how much
               More
                  Do you
                        Need.
```

Wendy and I have attended the Sun Valley Writers' Conference
since its inception. In 2019, TypewriterRodeo poets were there—
give them a word or phrase, and they'd bang out poems on vintage
typewriters. With the words *more to life than more*, Sean produced
this on a typewriter possibly as old as I was.

For my wife, Wendy, and our three children, Heidi, Lee, and Greg

I didn't expect to write a memoir in my eighties. And because of Lee, it became a different book from the one I set out to write. The story that emerged over the three years of writing and reflection has led me to a richer understanding of myself and my relationships with those I have loved. Particularly with Lee, who challenged me and who left us when he was so vibrant. I wonder what he would think, how he would feel, if he could read this book.

Chapter 1

Something's Wrong

We stood on the tarmac of the Boise airport, waiting in the dark. It was nearly midnight, and the last commercial flight had landed an hour ago. The airport was deserted. I had my arm around Wendy, and I could feel her shiver in spite of the warm summer night air and the heat still radiating from the surface of the airfield. The runway seemed to stretch out to the darkened landscape and the night sky beyond. It was one of those Idaho nights that is blacker than black and as wide as all the world.

Like me, Wendy was scouring the horizon for the incoming plane that would take us to New York. Every few minutes, she turned to look back at our son Lee lying on a gurney a few feet away, with his girlfriend, Criss, watching over him, a medical attendant standing nearby. We had no radio contact with the jet ambulance, now somewhere in that sea of black, en route from Reno, Nevada. All we knew was that it should be arriving around midnight and that time was critical.

Two days earlier, August 29, 1995, had started as a perfect day in Ketchum, the neighboring town of Sun Valley. Nothing unusual—*just another day in paradise,* as the locals like to say. We are used to impossibly beautiful days in the high desert mountains of Idaho, where the summers are warm and dry, never scorching. We fall asleep under puffy blankets, wake up to crisp mornings, recreate under cloudless skies, and watch the sun setting over the mountains at around 10 p.m. We are spoiled, perched in our pristine, pollution- and traffic-free bubble 6,000 feet above sea level.

That morning, I was as content as I'd ever been—and it was about more than just the beautiful day or the rush of the Big Wood River below my home office window. As a family, we had been blessed with good fortune, and the year 1995 started out as good as any we'd experienced. Earlier in the year, Wendy and I, in our 35th year of marriage, had cycled 600 miles together from Hanoi to Saigon—an extraordinary journey, even when counted among the many adventures we had already shared. Our daughter, Heidi, had just announced that she was expecting her first child—our first grandchild. Greg, our youngest, had been accepted at his choice of graduate business schools (my alma mater) and would be starting there in the fall.

And Lee, our middle child, had never seemed happier. His path had always been the rockiest of our three kids. But in the past couple of years, Lee seemed to be finding a good place in life, too. Now at the age of thirty, he was in love with a lovely young woman, and he had started a business in Ketchum that was thriving—The Buckin' Bagel, the first of a chain of stores that had recently expanded to Boise.

Sure, we had our everyday gripes and aggravations. For me, it's usually the small stuff that puts me over the edge—a fuse that repeatedly blows out in the house, a dripping faucet that I have no idea how to fix, or having to tear the house apart to find my lost keys, again. I'm known to be level-headed in a crisis, but leaving a good book behind on the airplane with the last chapter unread can ruin my day.

Just a few weeks earlier, Wendy repeated something we often said to each other: "Life has been good to us."

That tuesday afternoon, the 29th, I was on the phone in my office with an old friend who had been the director of a human rights organization I had chaired in the '70s when Wendy interrupted and motioned to me. She's not one to come bursting into a room, and looking at her face, I knew something was not right. She wasted no time. "Something's wrong with Lee. I need you right away," she said. "He's upstairs lying down. He had a car accident. He's fine, I think, but he just doesn't seem right."

Driving home from the neighboring town of Hailey, Wendy had noticed the flashing lights of a police car attending to a minor accident on the other side of the road. Then she saw that one of the cars was Lee's. She turned around and pulled over to see what was going on. The policeman told her Lee had tailgated and run into the car ahead of him; fortunately, he had been driving slowly enough that neither he nor the other driver appeared to be injured, other than a few scratches and bruises. The policeman confirmed that everyone was all right, but he thought Lee was acting a bit strangely.

"It might just be the cut on his head. Better keep an eye on him," he cautioned, "in case he has a concussion or something."

Lee insisted he was fine and told Wendy he wanted to take his car straight to the body shop a few miles down the road. She agreed to follow him in her car and then drop him off at his condo. On the way to the body shop, however, Lee's car kept drifting outside his lane. Alarmed, Wendy honked her horn a couple of times to get his attention. At the body shop, Lee remembered that all of his insurance information was at his apartment, but by the time he and Wendy got back to his place to look for the papers, Lee couldn't remember why they were there.

"Come on, Lee," Wendy said, trying to remain calm. "I'm taking you to our house now to see Dad." She gently steered him back to the car.

I sat next to Lee on the couch. Other than the scratch on the top of his forehead, he looked OK. While I talked to him and inspected the superficial wound, he was subdued and seemed a little lost. I wasn't too worried, but Wendy insisted we get him checked out.

Within a few minutes, we were on our way to the Moritz Hospital in Sun Valley, which was only two miles from our home. Lee was admitted right away to see the emergency room doctor on call. One of the benefits of living in a small town with a community hospital is that you usually get in without the interminable delays customary at big-city hospitals. The Moritz, built in 1961, was a little worn around the edges but had a comfortable and familiar feel to it. Many of Lee's friends had been born there; our son Greg had his appendix taken out there.

After examining Lee, the ER doctor didn't seem concerned but, as a precaution, suggested a CT scan for the bang on his head. "He'll be fine,"

I assured Wendy. Lee was in good hands, and I was sure we'd soon have confirmation that it was nothing worse than a slight concussion.

A half an hour later, the doctor came out to speak with us, his face the color of ash, his voice cracking at the edges. "Your son, I'm sorry to tell you, has a large tumor at the base of his brain."

ALL PARENTS DREAD getting bad news about their children. We've seen the unthinkable happen to other people, to friends and neighbors, but no one ever really believes it will happen to them.

For me, no relationship was as complicated as the one I had with my middle child. And when *that* is the child whose life is suddenly, inexplicably, at risk—at far too young an age—the process of coping and grieving can become even more knotted and convoluted.

Lee had been the most challenging of our three children. To be fair, it couldn't have been easy for him to be sandwiched between two siblings who were "model" children. Heidi and Greg were uncomplicated kids, motivated students, and good athletes. Lee was different. He wasn't by any means a bad kid—he was bright, sweet, witty, and very well-liked. But Lee could also be obstinate and mischievous and, frankly, a pain in the ass at times. He knew how to push people's buttons—especially mine.

In our family, we placed a high value on achievement, and Lee stood out with his struggles at school and in athletics. Wendy and I were often frustrated: our son was smart and physically strong, and we couldn't understand why he wasn't performing to his apparent abilities. I don't remember ever telling Lee I was disappointed in him. But I *know* he sensed it. "You don't have to say anything, Dad," Heidi has said to me more than once. "We know what you're thinking,"

The most challenging people in our lives, it's been said, can become our greatest teachers.

THOSE FIRST TERRIBLE words dropped on us by the doctor at the Moritz Hospital left us reeling. We heard what he said but couldn't make sense of it. Questions swirled in my head—questions I was, at that moment, incapable of asking the doctor: Is it cancer? What's *large*? What happens now?

Where did it come from? Will he be OK? The possibility of Lee dying never entered my mind.

"Lee probably blacked out while he was driving. That's what must have caused the accident," the doctor said. "I've already called to schedule him for an MRI tonight at Saint Alphonsus Hospital in Boise." His sense of urgency was palpable. "We don't have an MRI facility here, and in any case, you'll have to meet with a neurosurgeon."

It was now five o'clock, and Boise was a two-and-a-half-hour drive away. We raced home, threw some clothes in a bag for Lee and ourselves, and took off for Boise.

Boise is 150 miles from our home in the Wood River Valley, and in 1995 there wasn't a red light the entire way after you passed through the town of Hailey, ten miles down the road. Most of the drive is across wide-open camas prairie on a two-lane road that slices through the rural landscape like a fine crack in a piece of china. Over the years, I must have driven that route a hundred times, and I always went at least ten miles over the speed limit. I drove much faster that night.

I have no memory of what the three of us said to one another at the Moritz Hospital, nor the words Wendy and I might have spoken in the car as we barreled through the dusky landscape to Boise. We were in a state of shock, just trying to fathom what the hell was happening. The only thing I remember about the drive is that Lee slept the whole way, stretched out on the backseat. He said not a word.

It didn't occur to me that Lee's ability to communicate with us might soon be coming to an end.

THE LAST LENGTHY conversation we'd had with our son was a week earlier. Wendy and I, Lee and his girlfriend, Criss, and Heidi and her husband, Rick, were having dinner at Galena Lodge. Galena is in the middle of an alpine idyll twenty miles north of Ketchum. An historic, cozy cabin rooted in the mining history of Idaho, Galena caters to cross-country skiers in the winter and hikers in the summer. We had been on a guided wildflower walk earlier that evening, had finished dinner, and were just looking at the dessert menu. Lee, I noticed, had dropped the menu on the table with a frown.

"What's the matter?" I asked. "No dessert for you tonight?"

"No—I'm having trouble reading the menu. Everything's sort of blurry."

Even in the dimmed lights of the cabin, I could see that Lee's face was puffier on the left side and that his eye was slightly closed, as if, perhaps, he was suffering from allergies. Wendy also noticed, but neither of us said anything. We had had many conversations with Lee about his health that summer.

Lee hadn't been feeling well for a few months and had already been to see a number of doctors. Before Wendy and I left for Vietnam in late January, he thought he had the flu. When we got back four weeks later, he was still feeling crummy and was tired a lot of the time. In June, Greg and Lee went on a weeklong biking trip to Moab, Utah. Greg would be heading off to grad school at the end of the summer, and this was the last chance the boys would have to be together for a while. Lee was a keen mountain biker, but once they got to Moab, Greg noticed that his brother was feeling out of sorts. One morning, Lee told Greg he just didn't feel up to getting out on the trails that day.

"Come on, Lee, let's do it," Greg urged his older brother. "We only have three days left together, and then I'll be gone for almost a year."

"Sorry," Lee said. "I just don't have the energy today."

The whole summer was like that for Lee. He was taking time off from work and, as we found out later from his business partner, had been "disappearing" for frequent naps. Lee underwent numerous tests and received medical opinions ranging from intestinal bugs to esophageal infections, low blood sugar, chronic fatigue, and even depression. None of them proved out. At a loss, the last doctor Lee saw decided to schedule him for an MRI. It was two days before the MRI appointment that Lee had the car accident.

As SOON AS we arrived in Boise that night, we checked Lee into Saint Alphonsus's (St. Al's, to the locals). Wendy stayed there with him while I tried to find a hotel room for us. Boise was a small city—more of a big town, really—and wasn't exactly a happening place in the 1990s. That night, however, there wasn't a room to be had—perhaps it was the annual potato convention or something of the kind. Every hotel and motel was fully booked. After some scrambling, I finally found a motel catering to truckers; one room was left, having been held for a guest who didn't show up. I grabbed it and raced back to the hospital, arriving just as Lee was coming out from his MRI.

The news was bad. The neurosurgeon who sat down with us to go over the results explained that the base of Lee's brain was filled with fluid in the area surrounding the tumor. Lee, he insisted, should have surgery within the next three days at the very latest to relieve the pressure on his brain and spinal cord. There was no time to waste. Lee's life depended on it. The doctor proposed doing the surgery the following day.

I guessed the neurosurgeon was in his midthirties. As I listened to him, I tried to calculate how many operations this young man could have possibly performed so early in his career. I confess that his ponytail and beard didn't inspire me with additional confidence. Totally unfair, I know, but he was talking about going into our son's brain. And for all we knew, there might only be one chance to get it right. I wanted to make sure we were making the best choice for Lee.

Wendy and I thanked the surgeon, sat with Lee until he was asleep, and then planned the phone calls we would make early the following morning to family and friends and anyone and everyone we knew who might be qualified to advise and guide us on this road into the unknown. The unspoken certainty between us was that it was going to be terrifying. The last twelve hours already seemed like an eternity, and we were exhausted.

Wendy and I knew next to nothing about cancer, and we had never known anyone who had had a brain tumor. But it didn't take much imagination to figure out that a brain tumor is probably one of the worst types of cancer one could have. After spending hours on the phone with family members and close friends, we zeroed in on Hank Harris, a longtime friend and pediatrician to our three children; Wendy's brother Peter, who is an anesthesiologist in Vermont; her brother Michael, who had a contact at Sloane Kettering Hospital; and our friends Mort and Suzanne Marvin, who had a close friend who was a highly respected physician at NYU Medical Center.

By late Wednesday afternoon, these discussions and our frenzied research ultimately led us, through the Marvins' friend, to Dr. Patrick Kelly, Head of Neurosurgery at NYU Medical Center. He was widely recognized as one of the best surgeons in the field of neuro-oncology; he was also a pioneer of stereotactic surgery and had previously been at the Mayo Clinic before taking the helm at NYU Medical Center (now called the NYU Langone Medical Center).

But time was working against Lee: Dr. Kelly was scheduled to leave town in two days' time for the Labor Day weekend. When I reached him on the phone (itself, a miracle), I quickly filled him in. He agreed to see Lee if we could get him to New York City by early Friday morning. How would we get Lee from Boise to New York City in just over 24 hours?

THAT EVENING, WE took a break from the dozens of phone calls we had made that day. Each call to a friend or family member, each retelling of the unthinkable news about Lee, took us back to ground zero. Every conversation became a reliving of the last 24 hours. We tried to respond as best we could to the bewildered questions of people who loved Lee, and we found ourselves comforting others while we, too, were totally distraught.

To our surprise, the doctor agreed to let us take Lee to dinner at a nearby Chinese restaurant, as long as we got him back to the hospital within two hours. Criss had driven from Ketchum to Boise that afternoon to be with him, and Lee's business partner, Austin, had also come. Although Lee was able to walk on his own, he was weak and not very communicative. Most gut-wrenching for us was the distant look in his eyes, as though he weren't really there. The mass that had been slowly growing in Lee's head—for how long, we had no idea—was now visibly accelerating in its mayhem. Added to the memory loss, fatigue, and blurry vision, Lee was now also experiencing a loud and disorienting ringing in his ears and disruptive fits of hiccuping.

We tried to have as normal a dinner as the five of us could muster. For our family, Chinese restaurants have always meant comfort food. When we were raising the kids in Connecticut, Chinese takeout had been a Sunday night ritual. That night in Boise, there was no comfort to be found.

AFTER WE BROUGHT Lee back to the hospital that evening, Wendy and I jumped back into the race of figuring out how to get Lee to New York in time for the examination with Dr. Kelly. Boise didn't have a major airport; the entire population in the state of Idaho barely topped a million at that time. The most direct route we could find was to fly from Boise to Chicago and then transfer at O'Hare for a flight to New York, which would get us there barely in time to meet with Dr. Kelly. To complicate matters, Lee was becoming more fragile by the minute, and we weren't even sure if he'd be able to walk the next day. And he was bigger than I; fit as I was, I knew I'd have problems lifting Lee in and out of a wheelchair. I had visions of us careening through O'Hare only to miss our connection.

I had to find a plane, a private charter if necessary. The head nurse on Lee's floor at St. Al's told us that what we really needed was an air ambulance: Lee would be far better off, she explained, if he could lie down for the five-hour flight, accompanied by a trained medical attendant.

By Thursday morning, I managed to locate an available air ambulance 500 miles away, in Reno, Nevada. The flight coordinator I had on the phone couldn't guarantee it, but he thought the plane could get to us by midnight that evening. "But you'll need to decide quickly," he added.

"Can you hang on a minute, please?" I asked. I put the phone down and thought for a moment.

It was going to be tight. If we left Boise at midnight Mountain Time, we'd land at La Guardia at 7 a.m. Eastern, just in time for rush hour in New York City, which even under normal circumstances can be a sweaty-palm-inducing experience. Although we lived in Idaho, Wendy and I still had a place in the city and knew that arriving at one's destination on time is always a crapshoot. If we didn't get Lee to NYU Medical Center by 9 a.m., it would mean waiting another four days to see Dr. Kelly. Based on what the surgeon here was telling us, Lee didn't have that kind of time.

"This could be a life-or-death matter," I told the stranger on the phone, the words feeling surreal. "It can't be any later than midnight."

EVERY MINUTE WE waited on the tarmac felt like an eternity. Wendy and I stared at the sky, trying to distinguish the lights of an incoming plane from the stars, as if our looking would make the plane come sooner. Neither of us spoke. Although we couldn't make out the words, we could hear Criss murmuring as she bent over Lee, and Lee's sleepy voice mumbling in reply. Only many years later did Criss share with us what Lee had said in his few moments of clarity as he drifted between wakefulness and sleep and a place even farther away.

"I'm scared," he told her. "I love you. I want you to come with me to New York."

IT BROKE HER heart to tell him she couldn't go with him then. But Criss promised Lee she would come to New York as soon as possible.

SHE KEPT HER promise and, once there, didn't leave Lee until Lee left us.

Chapter 2

Father and Son

When Lee was in fourth grade, the head of his school asked to meet with us: Lee wasn't keeping up academically, and he was "acting out." Lee attended a prestigious day school in New Canaan, Connecticut, that catered to affluent families with a preponderance of high-achieving parents who expected the same of their children. Although the lower school was "ungraded," the students always knew exactly where they stood. Kids seem to have radar for that. The relaxed setting at the school was deceiving; the atmosphere was fiercely competitive.

Lee was fine in kindergarten but started to run into difficulties in first grade and fell further behind as he moved on. By the time Lee was eight, the headmaster informed us that he should go to a different school—one more suited to his abilities. "Lee is also immature for his age," the headmaster said. Then he added, with a slight smile, "But he'll probably outgrow that." *Preferably somewhere else* dangled, unsaid, in the air.

To me, it was coded bullshit for: *Your child doesn't measure up to our school; he's not smart enough.* Wendy and I balked at taking Lee out of the school. We knew he was *not* stupid. On the contrary—he was curious and intelligent; he just didn't fit neatly into the picture of the school's typical student.

On the advice of Lee's pediatrician, we took him to see a neurologist, who spent a few hours testing him.

"I understand you're a good athlete, Mr. Pesky," he said after we sat down in his office. "And I imagine you hoped that Lee would be, too."

I nodded. Sports was important in our family; I had made it important. I had always been a strong athlete, as were Wendy, Heidi, and Greg.

"Well, I've got news for you," the neurologist said. "He's not going to be. I've given Lee several tests—even simple ones, like asking him to walk a straight line—and it's clear that he has small motor difficulties that impede his coordination. It also shows up in his handwriting; it's virtually illegible, and he writes very slowly. That's probably why he's having difficulties at school."

And small motor difficulties were just one kind of challenge affecting Lee. He also had problems processing oral information, which compounded his struggles in learning. Basically, what Lee's brain was hearing and telling him wasn't necessarily what was coming out on paper when he wrote, the doctor explained.

"Lee's a bright kid," he assured us, "but you need to come to grips with the fact that these problems will never go away." For a child experiencing such challenges, the frustration can be overwhelming, the neurologist explained. Particularly when he is operating in an environment of high expectations.

My instinct was to jump in and challenge the doctor. "Yeah, but" was on the tip of my tongue. Instead, I kept my mouth shut and thought about what the doctor was telling us and how it related to what we had observed in Lee. The physical manifestations were, admittedly, the most noticeable. Lee *was* a bit klutzy—this was true. But his clumsiness was mixed in with a certain amount of grace. It was interesting (and puzzling) to watch Lee play baseball. He had great form, and he threw the ball beautifully. He also caught the ball nicely. But the bat rarely connected with the ball, and his running was ungainly. In tennis, he had beautiful strokes as long as the ball was hit right to him, but if he had to run for the ball, his game fell apart.

Lee's struggles in school made more sense now, too. Processing challenges (call it "internal wiring," if you will) are all but invisible, so disappointing results are easily misinterpreted as the kid just not trying hard enough. That was certainly my fallback assumption with Lee. I would eventually come to understand, though, that my misreading of Lee lay at the heart of my rocky relationship with him. But I would see that only after I learned considerably more about the hidden challenges Lee had faced.

The term "learning disabilities" (now also referred to as "learning differences") was first used at an educational conference in Chicago in 1963 by psychologist Samuel Kirk.[1] But it took about 20 years and two acts of Congress before awareness and meaningful support for learning disabilities began to trickle through to the front lines of education. One of the first milestones was the Children with Specific Learning Disabilities Act in 1969—the first federal law to mandate support services for affected students. The Individuals with Disabilities Education Act (IDEA) passed in 1975 required free "appropriate" public education for all kids with disabilities, and it was updated a number of times in the 1990s to expand access and protections for students with learning disabilities.

These were significant steps, but they were too late for Lee and others of his generation. In the early 1970s, the term "learning disabilities" was still largely unfamiliar to the general public, and scientific understanding of how the brain functions during the learning process was, for the most part, in the Stone Ages. The analytic and diagnostic capabilities we have now did not exist when Lee was "diagnosed"—so even with the neurologist's report, we only had a dim understanding of what Lee was dealing with. There was no way for anyone to know precisely which connections in Lee's brain were misfiring, and, therefore, it was impossible to come up with targeted solutions.

The neurologist went on. "There are some things you can do that might help your son compensate for his difficulties," he said. First, he suggested we find a learning specialist who could work with Lee. "Lee should also learn how to type so he won't have to struggle with doing papers and homework by hand," he said.

This was well before the time when computers had become a fixture in most households, and I was skeptical whether Lee, with his small-motor issues, could cope with typing. In fact, he never did learn to use a typewriter.

We did find someone who could meet with Lee every week to help him with his studies. We also took the neurologist's evaluation to Lee's school. The staff agreed to keep Lee enrolled and made some accommodations for him based on the doctor's suggestions. Because of his auditory processing challenges, for example, Lee was moved to the front of the classroom, an arrangement he initially balked at, not wanting to draw more attention to his challenges. But once he realized the move helped him to better hear and understand his teacher and take notes in class, he went along with it.

With some assistance, Lee was able to muddle through school. But, for Lee, the concrete benefits of the "fixes" were very limited—it was like slapping a Band-Aid on a wound that wouldn't heal. As far as the school was concerned, Lee was simply a problematic, underperforming student, and neither the neurologist's report nor our requests made them see Lee in a different light. To be fair, educators at that time did not have the means to recognize learning disabilities, much less know how to help students who were affected. They simply lumped all such children into the same category—"slow"—not realizing that learning disabilities indicate nothing about someone's intellectual capacity.

Meanwhile, the "specialist" who met with Lee weekly was really nothing more than a tutor. She could point out where Lee's work needed improvement, but she had no idea how to help him deal with his learning issues. She was not specially trained or educated in learning remediation.

Students with learning disabilities at that time were mislabeled and misunderstood. Just about everything that's available now to help kids navigate their learning disabilities to become thriving learners didn't exist then. Today, kids like Lee can get accurate diagnoses of their specific learning issues and intervention plans grounded in science. Remediation sessions with qualified specialists can help kids develop effective strategies for harnessing their strengths and working around their learning differences. And expert counseling is available now, too, to help kids and their families deal with the stress, anxiety, and other challenges that often accompany learning disabilities.

But unfortunately, the solutions recommended for kids like Lee in the 1970s and early '80s sometimes made matters worse. Learning disabilities were frequently misattributed to intellectual impairments or psychological problems. Even parents like us who were lucky enough to have the resources to try to find help for their kids were often grasping in the dark. They got whatever advice they could—some of it good, some of it useless, and some of it harmful.

Our pediatrician advised us to take Lee to see a child psychiatrist. Lee *hated* it. Every time we left the house for one of his early morning sessions, he would yell, "I don't want to go and see that man! I don't like him. I don't like what he's asking me!"

It was heart-wrenching then, and it's even more heart-wrenching now. When I hear Lee's panicked voice in my mind, I do so with the knowledge of how pointless and damaging those sessions were for him. The psychiatrist approached Lee's treatment as if he had a personality or mental disorder, rather than a processing issue that affected Lee's performance relative to his ability. What a message that must have sent to Lee: *You're all messed up.*

Back then, guesswork played a big part in figuring out what to do for a kid like Lee. In retrospect, any benefits he might have gained from the sessions with the psychiatrist were far outweighed by the negative impact that underlying message had on him. What a terrible, terrible decision it was on our part.

TODAY, LEARNING SPECIALISTS will tell you a simple and heartbreaking truth: The biggest problem with a child who has a learning disability isn't the child. It lies with those around the child—parents, teachers, family, friends—who don't understand why this kid is having problems. Collateral damage can be inflicted unwittingly by parents through the questions we ask or the advice we give to our children. Questions that are embedded with doubt and blame: *What's the matter with you? You're not paying attention. The problem is your attitude. Why aren't you studying more? You're not trying hard enough. Go back to your room and don't come out until the math problem is done.* When I was saying things like that to my son, it never occurred to me how pointless and damaging my words were.

We now know that 15–20% of the population, regardless of socio-economic or ethnic background, experience symptoms of a learning disability and that learning differences can occur across a wide spectrum in the degree of severity and type of disability. These disabilities are a matter of processing and should not be confused with developmental or intellectual impairments. They make the learning of basic skills like reading, writing, and math more difficult for some students when traditional, one-size-fits-all teaching approaches are used.

If you Google "famous people with learning disabilities," you'll come up with a surprising and diverse list of prominent people—Charles Darwin, Agatha Christie, Leonardo da Vinci, and George Washington, for example.[2] More recently, the list includes Richard Branson, Charles Schwab, Whoopi Goldberg, Richard Engel, Keira Knightly, and Anderson Cooper.

But unfortunately, there are far more people with learning disabilities who aren't thriving or famous. Learning disabilities not only slow you down in the learning process, they can also interfere with important life skills, such as time management and organization, long- or short-term memory, and attention. It's not surprising then, that these hidden challenges can have consequences beyond schooling. They can negatively impact relationships and one's ability to lead a fulfilling life.

OF COURSE, WE knew none of this when Lee was a child. If Wendy and I were vaguely aware of what his learning issues entailed, then Lee was totally in the dark about it. He knew only that certain things were hard for him without really understanding why.

Lee was not identified or defined by his disabilities. He was an active, impish, fun-loving, sweet, and somewhat unruly kid. That said, it's impossible to disentangle the essence of Lee from the fallout of his learning challenges. Over time, though, we came to understand that the frustration Lee experienced in dealing with his issues made him more apt to resist and rebel. And I have no doubt now that the disappointment he must have sensed in the people around him fueled Lee's inclination to provoke the perfectionists and Type-A people in his life. The most obvious target was me.

It annoyed me to no end at the time. Today, I have to admire how good Lee was at "poking me in the eye." But the prankster in him was always tempered by another side—a sweetness and tenderness that could take your breath away. When Heidi was pregnant with her first child, Lee bent down to kiss her belly as we were leaving a restaurant in Ketchum. "Hi, baby," he whispered. "It's your Uncle Lee." Eliza Lee Worcester was born just a few weeks before Lee died.

Lee was never mean. When he was a kid, though, he sure could stir things up. He liked to needle Heidi; she was, after all, the older sister and a by-the-book kind of sibling. As her cousin Mark observed, Heidi was the teenager who went to bed at 9 p.m. on New Year's Eve. She was a tough act to follow, and she'd often try to boss her younger brother around. "I don't need another mother!" Lee would shout at her.

He loved to throw his older sister off balance—literally, sometimes. And it counted as a double-header if he could get me riled up at the same time. Like on the day in 1978 when we were finishing a wonderful family hike to Kane Lake in the Pioneer Mountains of Idaho. Only twenty miles from Sun Valley and a world away from the frenetic pace of our lives on the East Coast, Kane Lake is one of the hundreds of pristine alpine lakes dotting the Idaho wilderness. The trail takes you through wildflower meadows and spruce forests, over icy creeks and ankle-busting scree fields. We were all good hikers, and after the 1,700-foot elevation gain, hearts pounding, we were rewarded in the last hundred yards of the climb with the sight of the turquoise lake just over the ridge below us. Utterly content, the five of us settled down in silence for a bite to eat, relishing the view and the sun on our faces. This is one of the many reasons why our family loved Idaho. After one more last deep breath of high mountain air, we hiked the three miles back down to our car. What a perfect hike and a perfect day.

That is, until we got down to the final stream crossing near the trailhead. It was late June, barely the start of summer in the 11,000-foot peaks, and the spring runoff from the snowmelt was still high. By late summer, the stream becomes a creek that hikers can easily hopscotch across. That day, however, we had to shimmy across a log perched over the ice-cold rushing water—the same way we had come when we started the hike.

I suggested Lee go first. For a kid who wasn't especially coordinated, he made it across OK. Heidi was next, and as she made her way along the wobbly log, Lee casually began tossing rocks into the stream below her to distract his sister. The stream was not especially deep, nor was it a big drop down from the log. But no one wants to fall in and do the drive home in wet boots. By the time she had crossed, Heidi was ready to kill her brother, and I was on the opposite bank yelling and waving my arms (have I mentioned I have a bit of a temper?). I was so worked up as I shuffled across that I nearly fell off the log myself.

Sputtering and fuming, I lectured Lee as I steered our car down the hairpin turns of Trail Creek Summit on our way back home to Ketchum. Imagine a narrow and winding dirt road carved into the side of a mountain. There are no guard rails. The passage is so steep and prone to avalanches that the road remains closed for about six months a year in the winter because it can't be plowed. That, however, didn't stop me from turning around now and then, white-knuckled hands gripping the wheel, to glare at my middle child who was looking innocently out the window. Greg, the peacemaker, had placed himself between his brother and sister in the backseat of the car.

Beside me, Wendy was alternating her attention between the drama in the car and the 800-or-so-foot drop-off to her right. "Alan, for God's sake! Keep your eyes on the road. We're all going to die!"

For many years, I viewed it as just another example of Lee being difficult. *No wonder I get pissed off at Lee*, I'd grumble to myself. But at some point, I turned the mirror back on myself. Lee was just being a kid; I, the adult, was being a jerk—quick to judge him harshly and lose my temper. When I'm being honest with myself, I know that had Greg been the one to throw stones to distract his sister, I would not have reacted in the same way.

Now we laugh about it. Well, it might be more accurate to say that Wendy, Heidi, and Greg roll their eyes about my performance in the Kane

Lake episode. When Heidi and her family go on that very same hike, one of her kids will inevitably ask, "Is this where Uncle Lee tried to make you fall in?" Naturally, we never told them the scary part of the story—the part when Pop Pop (the name my grandkids have given me) kept turning around on the hairpin turns to shout at Lee. That part was too terrifying.

KNOWING WHAT I know now, I've tried again and again to imagine what it must have felt like for Lee to be misunderstood and blamed for something he could do nothing about. Like most kids, he wanted to do well, and he tried hard to meet his own expectations and those of others—teachers, coaches, and his family. He was constrained, however, by disabilities he couldn't possibly understand.

What might that feel like? To understand *what* you need to do, and to know, in principle, *how* it should be done—but simply *not be able to accomplish it*? Would it be akin to knowing exactly what you want to say, but having the words come out of your mouth scrambled? Or concentrating as hard as you can to read a sentence but finding the letter order makes no sense at all, or that it changes every time you look at it? Like someone is messing with a switch in your brain?

I am unhampered by a learning disability—or any disability, for that matter—and it was difficult for me to understand why hard work just wouldn't pay off for Lee. It's not that everything came easily for me—because it didn't, particularly in academics. But in most other areas of my life, whenever I set a goal for myself, I knew I'd have a good chance of achieving it if I came up with a reasonable plan, if I was disciplined, and if I worked my butt off. I was driven, and I could make things happen. So naturally, I believed everyone else could do the same, if only they just put their minds to it.

At some point, Lee probably figured out that my approach, which I so frequently and pointlessly tried to foist on him, wasn't going to work for him. For me, the understanding was much slower in coming.

When Lee was eleven, he had to write a paper at school, *What I want to be when I grow up*. Lee didn't show me his essay, but Wendy did. "I want to be an advertising executive who also climbs mountains," he wrote. Or something to that effect.

Lee wanted to be like me.

It breaks my heart now when I think of it, because I, too, wanted him to be more like me. That longing—for Lee to strive, to score goals, to be a winner—kept me from loving my son as he was.

Chapter 3

What Does Love Look Like?

The plane seemed to move slowly through the midnight sky. Inside, it was dusk, the cabin lights dimmed. Wendy's eyes were closed, but I could tell she was not sleeping. Across from us, Lee was motionless, strapped into the narrow hospital bed. I tried not to think of all the things that could still go wrong during our race to get to NYU Medical Center in time to meet with Dr. Kelly: a flight delay, a holiday weekend traffic snarl, a sudden worsening of Lee's condition as fluid continued to build up in his brain. The possibility of arriving at the hospital only to find Dr. Kelly already gone for the Labor Day weekend was terrifying. When the pilot announced a couple of hours after takeoff, "We're on schedule for a 7 a.m. landing at La Guardia," I took a deep breath, closed my eyes, and thanked the God I didn't believe existed.

I peered out of the window but could see nothing from our capsule in the dark—no lights, no sign of life in the landscape below. My eyes were drawn back to Lee and the green-blinking monitor attached to his arm. Is this what love looks like? Most of the time, love is the day-to-day stuff: being there, providing a foundation, letting your child just be. But love can also be an unimaginable part of parenthood—finding yourself doing everything in your power to save your child's life.

I watched the rise and fall of my son's chest.

AFTER LEE BECAME ill, my thoughts often turned to my father. There was one moment in particular. My dad and I were walking through a long tunnel. It was cool and dark and damp. A jostling wave of people, all taller than I, pulled us along. I was excited, bursting with anticipation. When we poured out of the tunnel, and my eyes adjusted to the bright sunshine, I found myself looking onto a green sea of fresh-cut grass surrounded by bleachers reaching to the sky. I was six years old, and it was my first visit to Yankee Stadium.

It's impossible to describe just how big that place felt—like a new world opening up to me. From where we stood, just behind home plate, my eyes first went to the soaring flagpole at the far end of the stadium. Then the colorful billboards clamored for attention with their messages for Burma-Shave and Ballantine Beer. Beyond left and center field, I could see the elevated subway platform carrying the trains with people pouring out like ants, all coming to see the game. And framing the subway platform were apartment buildings, where surely the luckiest of fans lived. With binoculars from their living rooms, they could watch the action on the ballfield while listening to Mel Allen's gripping play-by-play account on the radio. The "Voice of the Yankees," Mel Allen could transport you from your home to the field, leaving your imagination to fill in the rest. In a voice brimming with exuberance, he'd describe a home run—his narrative punctuated by the cracking sound of the ball hitting a hickory bat—and finish off with a *Going, going, going, gone. Another Ballantine Blast for Joe DiMaggio!*

A few years later, television would take over that role and bring the excitement of baseball into everyone's home, but for me, it could never come close to capturing the magic of being at Yankee Stadium with my father in our fifty-cent bleacher seats, watching the likes of Joe DiMaggio, Lou Gehrig, Charlie Keller, Bill Dickey, and Red Rolfe.

Yankee Stadium was the crown jewel of New York and the heart of the Bronx, and it was just over a mile from our home. It was the biggest landmark of my childhood, with its narrow, dark tunnel to its expansive promise.

NOT LONG AGO, Wendy and I were at a dinner party in Sun Valley. "Where are you originally from?" the elegant woman sitting across from me asked in a slightly bored tone.

Usually, my accent gives it away. "I was born in the Bronx and spent my early childhood there; and later, in Queens," I responded. (I happen to be stubbornly proud of the place where I was born.)

"Really. The Bronx?" she said, after a pause.

"Really," I replied.

"Oh." She then turned to the dinner guest on her left, ending our conversation.

I get that a lot. The boroughs have enjoyed mixed reputations over the years, especially when compared with the glamourous veneer of Manhattan. They might be perceived by some as gritty next to the leafy cushiness of New York's upscale suburbs, like Stamford, Connecticut, where Wendy and I raised our kids. Heidi, Lee, and Greg were more privileged and sheltered in their youth than my brother and I were. They went on family vacations with us, played in tennis clubs, and enjoyed a pool in the backyard of our home. Yet, early one morning, just outside our idyllic suburban Stamford home, I found a swastika painted on our driveway. It was a chilling and unsettling reminder that no matter where you live, there are certain things you won't be shielded from. I don't think I've ever felt as violated as I did at that moment. Before Wendy and the kids could go outside, I called my best friend. He came right over, and without saying a word, we painted over the mark.

I HAD A more modest start to life than my children did, but the Bronx of the 1930s, like Queens, where we moved when I was eight, was as good a place as any to come from. For me, it was heaven. The Grand Concourse, Poe Park (as in "Edgar Allan"), Yankee Stadium, the Kingsbridge Armory and Reservoir, and Loews Paradise Theater—these are the treasures of my childhood memories.

Loews Paradise was aptly named. It opened its doors in 1929, a month before the Great Crash—fortuitous timing, as movie theaters were a godsend for many during the Depression. The lobby was absurdly ornate with its gilded moldings and painted murals. But the real magic happened inside the 3,800-seat theater. If you could tear your eyes from the giant screen long enough to look up, you would see the night sky moving above, ingeniously projected onto the ceiling of the theater. The North Star might be rising on your lower left as you walked in to take your seat and arcing to the upper right two hours later when you streamed out of the theater, fueled by Good & Plenty, Raisinets, and Tootsie Rolls.

Even better, if that's possible, was Krum's Ice Cream Parlor. If Joe DiMaggio was the greatest hitter who ever lived, then the man who served ice cream sundaes in gleaming tulip-shaped metal dishes was the greatest ice cream scooper who ever plied his trade. And a few doors down, at a little place whose name I've long since forgotten, we would get charlotte russes: sponge cakes nestled in little white cardboard holders and adorned with a mound of real whipped cream topped with a cherry. Perfect bliss. It was there that I discovered at the age of six the unparalleled delight of inhaling whipped cream through my nose.

The Bronx was a vibrant and thriving place, a microcosm of a country undergoing transformation and rebirth. After the First World War, people were thrown together like never before. Millions flowed into the largely rural borough from the more crowded parts of Manhattan; or, like my father, they came from other states, looking for work and a better life for their families. Irish, Germans, Italians, Jews, Poles, African Americans— each concentrated in their respective neighborhoods, yet overlapping in parks and schools, on playgrounds, and at work. A hard-working and ethnically diverse middle class eager to get ahead.[3] Among them were my parents.

I was born in 1933, which was by most historical accounts a terrible year. It was a low point in a catastrophic decade, bookended by a stock market crash and a war that we've not seen the likes of since. One out of four people was out of work, despair and suicide rates were spiking, and birth rates had plunged. The Depression doesn't spring to mind as an ideal time in which to have begun one's life. And for many, it wasn't. But my father had work, and our family was spared the devastating losses so many others endured.

From age eight to twelve, I experienced the world at war from a distance. The main impact on us was the rationing of everyday commodities that we tend to take for granted, like sugar, meat, and gas. But it didn't feel like deprivation to me because we were all coming together for a larger purpose: to help our country win the war. True, the rationing meant that I only occasionally got bubble gum, but I figured out how to get extra mileage out of every piece by sticking it onto the bedpost when I went to bed so I could enjoy it again the next day.

In some ways, my generation was among the luckiest. We came of age after the war ended when the doors to prosperity blew open. Money that had been diverted into the war now poured into new infrastructure, public education, and the GI Bill—booster shots for a country bursting with pent-up demand. My contemporaries and I benefited from one of the greatest periods of prosperity in American history, during which the middle class expanded and thrived like never before. It was a good time to test your wings, most particularly if you were White and male.

In a sense, the time and place in which I grew up felt like my very first view of Yankee Stadium—a thrilling expanse where anything was possible. Yet my home life as a child could feel like quite the opposite. I struggled in my relationship with my father, and I chafed at the predictability and sameness of my parents' lives. As adults, Wendy and I have always tried new things—trying different foods, going to avant-garde art exhibits, attending concerts, and seeking adventure on our vacations. As parents, we made a point of challenging our kids and introducing them to the wider world through travel and education—and we had the means to do so. We were both actively involved in their upbringing; I practically had a blueprint for how their lives should unfold. We discussed school assignments, grades, and activities with them and encouraged them to make a commitment to athletics. Once they were in high school, we talked with them about their summer jobs and how they might best prepare for college.

My parents took a decidedly more laissez-faire approach with us. Yes, they wanted my brother and me to go to college (I would be the first in our extended family to go), and they hoped we'd "make something" of ourselves. But filling in the details was left to us—the sports we chose to pursue, when and how well we did our homework, and, once we were older, how we'd get to school and which colleges we'd apply to. In this way, they gave us a great deal of freedom. Our parents provided what we needed; we didn't lack for anything. But at times, their largely hands-off approach felt like an absence—particularly when it came to my father. I wanted words, a hand on my shoulder, an occasional pat on the back. My father was there for us, but he wasn't really *there*, at least not in the ways I would have liked him to be.

My FATHER, LOU Pesky, was a working man whose formal education ended at high school. A reserved man, he shared no stories of his childhood and invited no questions. I knew next to nothing about his early life, other than the fact that he left school early to help support his family.

His limited formal schooling notwithstanding, our father was sharp and had a photographic memory for numbers and a quick ear for languages. In his low, gravelly voice, he conversed easily in Spanish and Yiddish with workers in the meat-packing district, where he was fondly known as "Big Louie," a nickname derived from his deep voice and considerable girth. With his 5'10", 250-pound frame and a nose that spread across his face, it was hard to see the handsome man he once was. Until he smiled. He had a smile that radiated warmth and could light up a room, revealing his good nature and a shy charm.

As well liked as he was in his work world, to me my father was a stranger. Our day-to-day upbringing was left almost entirely to our mother, which was not unusual for that time. Conversations with my father beyond the "pass the salt" variety were few, if nonexistent. He never asked my brother and me questions or spoke to us about our schooling, sports, or other activities—let alone politics, current events, or anything of a cultural nature.

He came only once to watch me play in a basketball game. I was in high school and cocaptain of the Jamaica High basketball team. I had no idea my father would be at the game, and he said nothing to me afterward. "Your father watched you play," my mother told me over her shoulder as she washed the dishes that night. "He's very proud of you." It killed me that he had said nothing to me himself. I didn't want to hear his praise secondhand.

To be fair, my father wasn't around very much because he worked long hours, six days a week, in a tough trade. When he first arrived in New York from Brockton, Massachusetts, he set himself up as a meat jobber—a small meat distributor—a trade that is now extinct. "I could do it myself" was his response when we asked why he'd chosen that particular occupation. He didn't want to work for someone else. Today, you might call him a "small business owner" or, if you were dressing it up a bit, an "entrepreneur." He viewed it as making a living to support his family. The business model, if he had one, was simple: buy a truck, rent a meat locker in a refrigerated warehouse, buy from slaughterhouses and meat processors, and sell to small butcher shops, corner groceries, and bodegas in Queens, the Bronx, and Harlem.

He woke every day at 3 o'clock in the morning and was at work by 4:30; twelve hours later, he would return home. My brother, Andy, and I both worked for our dad in the summers of our late high school and early college years. It was hard, dreary, mind-numbing work. My workday with my father and the handful of guys he employed would begin in the dark, unloading the trucks that brought the meat from his suppliers. I was neither treated nor viewed as "the boss's kid." I learned to pick up large wooden crates and cardboard boxes without destroying my back, some as heavy as 50 pounds. "Bend your knees when you pick them up, Alan, or your balls will drop to your toes," my father would warn. Then I'd hoist the boxes onto one shoulder and haul them into the warehouse for unpacking and sorting into the ice-cold locker. Later in the morning, the truck driver and I would begin our deliveries to bodegas and butcher shops all over the city.

The thought of following in my father's footsteps never entered my mind. I wouldn't have minded the brutal hours had it been a business that interested me. But I just couldn't see myself in the meat trade. I aspired to a different life from the one my father led. I wanted to wear a suit and a tie, live in the city, and travel abroad rather than go to Florida once a year. But those summers working for my father were invaluable. Although neither Andy nor I realized it at the time, we were absorbing a work ethic in the meat-packing district that would serve us well many years later in our respective careers—Andy in the travel industry, and I in advertising.

You wouldn't think that meatpacking and advertising had much in common, but what I learned in the former contributed to my advancement in the latter. Working with my father, I was just one of a mix of people from a wide range of professional experiences, educational backgrounds, and ethnicities. And none of these things mattered when it came to moving meat around. You learned to get along, respect one another, and get the job done. Some of our ad agency clients were a lot like the people I met when I worked for my dad—tough, savvy, unvarnished, and plain-spoken. Like Frank Perdue, the "tough man who raised the tender chickens," whose company was one of our more prominent accounts at Scali, McCabe, Sloves, the agency my partners and I founded. Frank was unpretentious and hard-nosed—a no-bullshit guy who flew economy and couldn't care less about the kind of suits he wore. He handled himself more like guys I'd met in the meatpacking business than the CEO of a multimillion-dollar corporation. He trusted me, and we became friends.

Today, I have tremendous respect for the work my father did. It was hard, and he did it well. But when I was a kid and then a teenager, the unvarying nature of his work life irked me—the same routine, six days a week, year after year. His business never got bigger and never got smaller, staying more or less the same for 25 years. That lack of variation carried over into my parents' home life in a Groundhog-Day kind of repetitiveness. Every day, when my brother and I got home from school, we'd find our dad dozing in the same easy chair in the living room with his feet on the ottoman, ashtrays strategically placed nearby to accommodate his three-pack-a-day habit of unfiltered Camels. The ashtrays were always spotless, cleaned by our mother with invisible efficiency and ruthless speed, even before the next Camel was lit. Every Sunday, after we moved to Queens, we'd go out for dinner to the same place, a kosher deli in Fresh Meadows called Harris's. Occasionally, the routine was broken by dinner at a Chinese restaurant (always the same one). I can still recite my dad's order at Harris's: a three-inch-thick sandwich with corned beef or pastrami (better yet, a combination of the two) and a side of coleslaw and potato salad, all washed down by Dr. Brown's Cream Soda (often referred to then as the Jewish version of Coke). The sandwiches were accompanied by a large plate of sour and semisour pickles, an essential part of a deli meal. Today, I shudder at his diet. My dad suffered from high cholesterol most of his life and died at the age of 59 from a cerebral hemorrhage, attributed by his doctor to his sky-high cholesterol and lack of exercise.

Exercise for the sake of physical well-being or participating in sports for fun did not appeal to my father, but watching and betting on games did. Lou Pesky loved to gamble. Bookies were a fixture in the meat business, and betting became a natural part of my father's life. He was on familiar terms with his bookie, "Solomon," to whom my father was simply "L.P." I would often hear my father on the phone, speaking in what sounded like code: "L.P. for Solomon. I'll go ten times on the Yanks." After coming home from the track, my father would toss a handful of colorful tickets on the hallway table. They were just orange, blue, and green scraps of paper to me, but to him, they were losing bets on horses. Unlike some of his friends, Lou never got into debt because of his gambling, at least that we knew of. I don't remember my mother ever speaking about it. Although my parents argued a lot—and my mom was more than a match for my father when it came to verbal sparring—she was uncharacteristically silent on the subject of his gambling.

Today, when I see pictures of my mother, Belle, as a young woman, I'm taken aback by how beautiful she was, with her jet-black hair and dark eyes. If not overly warm, she was a devoted mother, taking meticulous care of her family and putting three meals on the table every day. She had a driver's license but never drove, and she never considered working outside of the home, even after our father died and money was tighter for her. What stood out for me most about my mother when I was a child was her efficiency and neatness. She kept the house in pristine order (plastic furniture covers were essential in that endeavor) and was scrupulous with her appearance. When she left the house to meet her friends at Hadassah (the Jewish volunteer women's organization) or to play a game of canasta or mah-jongg, she was perfectly groomed and often wore a hat and a pair of gloves.

My mother's laser-like focus on neatness never wavered. When I was 42, our agency was featured on the cover of the *New York Times Sunday*

Magazine.[4] The photos for the article happened to be taken after Wendy and I had just returned with the kids from a Colorado river trip, on which I hadn't shaved. Excited and bursting with pride (I had gotten to the newsstand at 6 that morning to grab a stack of copies), I called my mom to tell her about the article. She took one look at the piece and called me right back. "My son finally gets his picture in the *New York Times*—and with that beard!" she said. "I can't even see your face."

My mother was not shy about sharing her opinions, but she knew how to keep a secret when it was important. My brother and I were stunned to find out, by chance, that our mother was our father's second wife. The word "divorce" had never been spoken in our home. And although my mother obviously knew about his first wife when she married him, she never publicly acknowledged that he'd been married before. Marrying a divorced man was frowned upon in her social circle. I suspect Belle and her acquaintances looked at it as "buying second-hand merchandise." Andy and I were in our late teens when we finally learned that the "Cousin Bernice" my father took us to visit on Sunday afternoons—while our mother waited in the car with a frozen look on her face—was our half-sister. Given my mother's views on the subject of divorce, I've often wondered why she married my father. They weren't affectionate with each other in our presence, and they fought a lot—but then, many married couples do. Did my parents love each other? Maybe. I really don't know. But it was not the kind of love I envisioned for myself.

Love can be a hard thing to recognize as a kid. Especially if you have parents, as I did, who are undemonstrative. My father didn't do many of the things I saw my friends' fathers doing, and which I interpreted as love, like tossing a ball with us out on the street or shooting baskets with me after school. But he did share a very important thing with me, and that was his passion for sporting events. Going to baseball games at Yankee Stadium and basketball games and prizefights at Madison Square Garden—these are some of the best memories I have of my dad. It was a gift from him that shaped me in a profound way.

The summer my father took me to my first baseball game also stood out for me because of a notable event in baseball history. On July 4, 1939,

Lou Gehrig gave a speech that many Americans consider the greatest sports speech of all time. The "Iron Horse" of baseball, who had played a record-breaking 2,130 consecutive games, stood at a microphone before 61,000 avid Yankee fans and announced his surprise retirement from baseball due to a cruel and devasting disease. I will never forget his opening words: "For the past two weeks you have been reading about a bad break. Today I consider myself the luckiest man on the face of the Earth."[5] Two years after this announcement, at the age of 37, Lou Gehrig died of amyotrophic lateral sclerosis (ALS), which became widely known as "Lou Gehrig's disease." There is still no cure.

I didn't know much about anything as a kid, but I knew this man was a hero. Not only because of his accomplishments on the field, but also for the way in which he chose to face his imminent death—as "the luckiest man on the face of the Earth." My admiration for his grace deepened over time, particularly when we faced the loss of our son, and I came to understand how much more there was to life than having more recognition, more achievements, more money.

These outings with my father to ball games not only exposed me to my first heroes, but they also stoked my passion for sports. I didn't just want to watch; I wanted to play. Once I discovered the basketball court down the street at P.S. 26 after we moved to Queens, I was hooked. I played there every chance I had, usually until dark. Kids from the surrounding neighborhoods converged on that court, and the competition was fierce. But I never once witnessed a fight or a major disagreement. If you were fouled, you called it, and the kid guarding you accepted it. I've seen more cheating in one round of golf than I ever did in my years on the P.S. 26 playground.

Every day, I would dribble my basketball down the street, showing off my skill to the neighborhood by bouncing the ball behind my back and through my legs as I made my way to the playground. It never occurred to me that my father noticed. But then, one afternoon, I came home from school to find a hoop attached to our garage. No fanfare. It was just there. From then on, I would be out there shooting baskets late into the night, every night, under the garage lights. The steady *thunk, thunk, thunk* . . .

swish! became the white noise of Pesky family evenings. To this day, I don't know how my father, who was in bed by 8 every night, could fall asleep to the incessant drumbeat of a basketball pounding on the driveway.

As a father and grandfather, I empathize with my dad for putting up with the noise, and I admire him for his trust in us. Regardless of what he thought of my obsession and all my other interests, he supported them. I was not as easygoing about Lee's choice of sports as my father was with mine. Once Wendy and I moved to Connecticut, we became a tennis family, and I was the biggest enthusiast. We belonged to two tennis clubs and even had a court on our property. Sunday evenings in the summer, the family would play doubles, vary the teams, and then all sit down in the backyard to a barbeque dinner, usually laughing about how Heidi had nearly decapitated me with her punishing forehand.

One summer, Wendy and I decided to send Lee to a marvelous (we thought) tennis camp in Vermont. Heidi had been there and loved it. A few days after our friend Mort dropped his son and Lee off at the camp, the phone rang. It was the boys: *We hate this place; we want to come home.* After much discussion, we decided to make our sons tough it out. The boys survived, of course, and ended up having a pretty good time.

But Lee continued to dig in his heels about tennis. The following summer, he announced that he wanted a dirt bike. I cringed. Intellectually, I got it. Even though Lee was a decent tennis player, his small-motor challenges would continue to make the sport difficult for him. Emotionally, though, I was resistant; there was a stubbornly hopeful part of me that still wanted to see my son playing in a tennis tournament. Tennis fit in with the lifestyle I had envisioned and cultivated for our family. A dirt bike didn't. Nobody in our circle of friends had a dirt bike. My vision was populated with F. Scott Fitzgerald-type characters wearing tennis whites, not dirt bike knee pads. Looking back, I can see how ridiculous it was. Who cares whether it's tennis, soccer, or a dirt bike? As long as kids are engaged and having fun.

But at the time, I did care, so I tried to talk Lee out of it. Nonetheless, he was determined to trade in his tennis duds for a mud-spattered bike. I gave in to my 15-year-old son's wishes with one proviso: Lee would have to pay for the bike by working it off over a period of time. I was skeptical, thinking (maybe hoping) it might just be a whim or a rebellious phase, so I insisted we make our agreement official. Off we went to the bank, Lee wearing a jacket and tie. We sat down with the bank manager, who shook hands with Lee and made up a loan coupon booklet for him: each monthly payment was for $25. But I had underestimated Lee, who remained committed to his new hobby. He worked long and hard and paid off every penny of the loan on time. My son loved riding his dirt bike, and I was proud of him for his determination. But I hated that damn bike.

Today, it wouldn't be an issue for me. In fact, I hope I would celebrate Lee's resistance, his drive to follow his passions instead of mine. Not because I particularly like dirt bikes any more than I did then, but because I've gotten over the part of myself that felt the need to present a certain image. I also see now what I didn't see then about Lee: He had the strength to stand up to me. *This is me. This is what makes me happy.*

IF MY IDEA for tennis camp for our kids went over like a ton of bricks with Lee, my father's decision to send his sons to summer camp was a stroke of genius. Many of my friends tell me they are still traumatized by their camp experiences. Wendy, too, was homesick all summer long at camp. Books have been written and movies made about summer camp, a vigorously debated American rite of passage. For me, it was a game changer.

I first attended Camp Barrington in West Copake, NY, when I was eight. My father had some friends in the meat trade who had sent their kids to this camp. One day at breakfast he turned to me and said, "Alan, you'll be going to camp this summer." No discussion or explanation. Before I knew it, I was on a bus heading to camp a few hours north of Queens. It was my first extended time away from home. I didn't know anyone and had no idea what to expect. I was terrified.

But I loved being outside, and the setting was irresistible. Surrounded by the Catskill Mountains and the Berkshires, Camp Barrington had everything a kid could want: fresh air, a lake, canoes, trees, cabins—you name it. Even better, it was all about sports. To my surprise and relief, I discovered within the first few days that I was good at softball and volleyball, two big sports at Barrington. I wasn't a prodigy, but I played well enough to stand out.

Finding that you are good at something when you're a kid (and realizing that other people notice it) can give you a sense of confidence and open worlds of possibilities. For me, it happened to be athletics, something that is still a huge part of my life, even at the age of 87. By now I've had to trade in my road bike for a stationary bike in spin class, where my presence raises the average age by at least a decade or two. And I've given up trail running for walking the golf course, where Wendy routinely clobbers me when we play. (I couldn't be prouder of how far she can hit the ball. Except when she tells our friends how much farther her ball goes than mine.) No more running marathons or climbing mountains for me, either. Although I did walk the New York City Marathon with Heidi in celebration of my 80th birthday.

It was at summer camp that I first realized I had a fierce competitive streak. For the most part, my competitiveness came through in a form of dogged perseverance, something that would serve me well in life. But from time to time it manifested in more traditional ways, and my younger brother, Andy, was usually on the receiving end.

By all accounts, I was not an ideal older brother to have. If I viewed my little brother as a pest (he was, after all, four years younger), Andy saw me, rightfully, as a bit of an asshole. Today, we couldn't be closer, and he is far too gracious to remind me of a little episode in which my competitive spirit might have gotten a bit out of hand.

One summer, when I was a junior counselor at Barrington and Andy was a young camper, we found ourselves on opposing teams in the end-of-summer, four-day competition known as Color War. In this annual tradition, kids were assigned to teams denoted by the camp's colors, blue and gold. Color War was serious business.

The competition in question was a basketball game between the Blue team (which I, as a counselor, was coaching) and the team Andy was playing on, Gold. Andy was not only the tallest kid in his group, but the best player on his team. As his brother, I knew all his moves and strengths. Operating on this inside information, I figured that if our team could neutralize Andy, we'd win the game.

"Look at that big guy out there," I said, pointing him out to my team. "You're going to have a problem holding him down." I lowered my voice and leaned in. "Okay. Here's our defense: Every time Andy gets the ball, you're going to swarm him."

They followed my instructions to a T, and we took Andy and the Gold team to the cleaners. It was not a good day for Andy, and it wasn't my finest moment. I'm not sure if he's ever forgiven me, but he loves me anyway.

Camp barrington opened my eyes to more than just sports. It was also the place where I discovered music. My parents didn't listen much to music at home and never went to concerts. So, I'm not sure why my mother insisted we take piano lessons—perhaps because she adored José Iturbi, a pianist and conductor who appeared in several movie musicals of the 1940s. But I was no Iturbi or Liberace. I had no talent, and I hated the lessons. It didn't help that the piano teacher had bad breath and yellow teeth and would put his face close to mine while he was pointing out something on the sheet music.

The summer I was a senior camper at Barrington, our camp director organized an outing to Tanglewood, the summer home of the Boston Symphony Orchestra. We spread our blankets on the lawn and, surrounded by the Berkshires, began to listen to the music. For me, it was as if I were *hearing* it for the first time. After the sky darkened and filled with stars, the orchestra moved on to its final piece, *The 1812 Overture*, which ended with bells ringing, cannons roaring, and an extravagant display of fireworks. Lying there that evening in 1947, listening to the strains of a Russian by the name of Tchaikovsky, my imagination was ignited.

I have been a lover of music ever since—classical, gospel, opera, you name it. That experience also made me hungry to try things I had never done, unfamiliar and challenging things. If this is what music under a night sky could feel like, just imagine what other adventures might be out there for me.

Why not? would become my lifelong motto. It's not particularly original, as others before me have had it. *Cur Non* was emblazoned on the family

crest of the Marquis de Lafayette, a hero of the French and American rev-
olutions. The college I attended, Lafayette, was named after him, and I'd
like to think I absorbed the spirit of his words while I was there.

CURIOSITY, CONFIDENCE, AND accomplishment—even in one small area
of your life—can be transformational. Add those ingredients to the era in
which I grew up, and you get an intoxicating mixture. That's how high
school was for me, where basketball and remarkable societal changes
converged. Jamaica High School in Queens was, at the time, the largest
high school in the country. It would also become one of the most highly
regarded public schools in the US, boasting many notable alumni. When
I was there, from 1947 to 1951, it was starting to benefit from desegrega-
tion measures and seeing a glimpse of its future glory days. The Supreme
Court's landmark decision in 1948 to strike down racially restrictive housing covenants brought more African American families to Queens, which,
like the Bronx, had still been quite segregated when I was a boy.

Author and writer Jelani Cobb, who is also an alumnus of Jamaica
High, wrote about the school in *The New Yorker* after Jamaica High closed
in 2014. One of the alumni he interviewed, John Ward, was a few years
younger than I. Ward described Jamaica, Queens, much as I remember it:
an ethnically diverse community where people, for the most part, got along.
For me, Jamaica High School was like that, too—a harmonious microcosm
of the societal shifts taking place across the country. Three years after I graduated, John Ward was elected as the school's first African American class
president. Ward told Jelani Cobb, "I don't really recall there being much
racial tension . . . The blacks mostly hung out with other black students,
but, being an athlete, I interacted with a lot more of the white students."
Cobb then writes, "For a few years in the fifties, Jamaica's integrated athletics teams, with their winning records, were a point of pride for the school."[6]

Ward's chosen sport at Jamaica High was baseball; mine was basketball. And basketball was king in New York, a city that dominated the sport
in the 1940s and '50s. Jamaica High School was a basketball powerhouse
in Queens, always one of the better teams in the city. And it benefited
from the diversity of its team. So did I.

I was chosen as cocaptain of the basketball team in my senior year. It wasn't because I was a particularly high-scoring player or, for that matter, nearly as good a player as my cocaptain, Leander Jones. In fact, I usually wasn't the most talented person in things I chose to pursue. But the advantage of not being "great" or "a natural" is that you always have to try harder. The tenacity I developed, along with my instinct for zeroing in to guard the best player on the opposing team, are probably why the coach picked me.

It felt like a big deal, as a 17-year-old, to be leading one of the top teams in the city. Never mind the fact that our team that year had the worst record in the school's history. As I like to say, the record book doesn't say "cocaptain of the worst team." And I was later comforted by the evidence that I hadn't ruined the team forever: a few years after I graduated, Jamaica High won the New York City High School Championships at Madison Square Garden. The city championship was a distinction that some might say was akin to winning the NCAA tournament today.

Most important, at Jamaica High School I was living the changes we were seeing in the broader world. Our basketball coach had chosen a Black kid and a Jewish kid to lead the team together. Leander Jones was my teammate, and I liked and admired him. Embracing the diversity I saw at school, I asked my parents one day, "Wouldn't it be nice if Leander and his parents could come over and have dinner with us?"

No, I was told. It would not.

Comments my parents made about African Americans made me uncomfortable even before I was old enough to articulate why. When I was a teenager, their biases pissed me off.

I left Queens to go to Lafayette College in Pennsylvania in 1951, only six years after the end of World War II. We could almost feel the ground shifting beneath us. Europe was rebuilding itself from the devastation of the war, the US had just entered the Korean War, and the Cold War was heating up. We marveled at the first direct-dial, coast-to-coast telephone call and the first nonstop flight around the world. A woman named Margaret Sanger was funding research for the first birth control pill around the same time that the US government began testing nuclear bombs in the Nevada desert. In Topeka, Kansas, a third-grader was denied entry to the elementary school nearest her home because she was Black, and her father filed a class-action lawsuit in federal court that would land at the Supreme Court and lead to the landmark decision known as Brown vs. Board of Education three years later. The early '50s marked the beginning of the Civil Rights era and the resurgence of the Ku Klux Klan.

As the world was battling to right itself, my contemporaries and I were beginning to write our own stories. It was a messy and unsettling time, exhilarating and ugly. But underlying everything, there seemed to be a sense of optimism and the opportunity for something better. That was my frame of mind when I left home. I was determined to get the very most out of life, challenge myself, and make my mark.

Children can be the harshest critics of their parents, and I was not gentle in my assessment of mine. Yes, I saw my parents as good people who worked hard and did the best they could for their children. But my eighteen-year-old self was embarrassed by what I viewed as their antiquated notions and lack of worldliness. I wanted more for myself. And at that time, "more" meant different from my father. I wanted to be more sophisticated, so I arrived at college wearing preppy clothes because that's what I thought sophisticated people looked like. I wanted to make more money, more than enough to support a family, see the world, and do the things I wanted to do. I wanted to get away from the monotonous, plastic-covered-furniture home life of my childhood. And once a father myself, I vowed I would always be available to my kids and actively involved in their lives.

An understanding of the gifts our parents have given us comes gradually. Much as I did with Lee, rather than notice what *was* there as a teenager and young man, I focused on what was missing in my relationship with my father: conversations, active guidance, praise, his presence at my ball games. In his personal qualities, I saw absences, too—of polish, formal education, any desire to lead a healthy lifestyle. On Parents' Weekend during my freshman year at Lafayette College, most of my friends' fathers arrived wearing suits—appropriate, I thought, to the importance of the occasion. My father, the meat jobber, showed up, stomach bulging, in an open-necked shirt.

As I got older, my embarrassment shifted from my parents to myself. I came to see them through the lens of who they were, not who I wanted them to be. What did love mean for my parents? I can't speak for them, but I can tell you what their love and parenting did for me: the home life they created, which I had perceived as humdrum and unexciting, provided me with a solid foundation. It was there that I learned about honesty and hard work, the importance of family, being there for one another day in and day out, and generosity—values I have tried to live up to all my life and that I've passed on to my children. Although Lou Pesky had had little exposure beyond his world and couldn't offer specific guidance on how we might better ourselves in our changing world, he always advanced the interests and ambitions of his sons, not with words or advice, but with actions. My dad was not wealthy, but he provided well for his family. I took this support for granted, and I didn't recognize it for the love it was until many years after both my parents were gone.

My father's lack of active intervention in our young lives was wiser than I gave him credit for. It forced me to be self-reliant, independent, and a self-starter. I took a different approach with my children. My involvement seemed to work well for Heidi and Greg (although Hope, one of our grandchildren, who happens to be a lot like me, has firmly asked me to back off on occasion). But perhaps my inclination to manage and plan wasn't the best approach.

Most of all, I wonder about Lee, how he perceived my parenting, what my love for him looked like from his perspective, because he isn't here anymore to tell me what he thinks.

When I got out of graduate school, Wendy and I moved into our first apartment in New York City, a small, middle-income co-op. One day, a few months after Heidi was born, the doorbell rang. It was my dad with a big smile on his face and arms loaded with meat. Wendy and I tried to find room in our small fridge for all the packages he'd brought, and my father got down on the floor and played for hours with Heidi, who adored her big, bear-like grandfather.

"Your father's such a lovely man," Wendy said, smiling, after he left.

Yes, he was.

But it was only after he was gone that I came to appreciate the way he expressed his love—with an armful of meats at the door, by taking me to ball games at Yankee Stadium, by showing up at Parents' Weekend at my college, where his pride of seeing me there overcame any discomfort he might have felt at being out of his element.

My father and I had a good conversation in 1981 when I was running the New York City marathon for the first time. I was 48, and my father had been dead for 20 years. I was about three-quarters of the way through the marathon and entering the Bronx segment of the course. I was not far from where my father had his business and where I worked summers for him when I was in college. Although the neighborhood had changed a lot, it was still intensely familiar to me. I was hitting the 20-mile "wall" and seriously doubting whether I would be able to power through to finish the race.

Then I found myself talking to my father. "C'mon, Lou, help me out here. I know you're there. I need help. Can you give me the strength to finish this?" True to form, my father didn't say anything. But he gave me what I needed.

Chapter 4

Love Lee

The MRIs were illuminated by a lightbox. A small group of us in Dr. Kelly's office gathered around the images. We were looking at Lee's brain. It could have been anyone's brain up there on the wall. But it was our son's, whose handsome face and playful smile were nowhere to be seen on these pictures.

OUR PLANE HAD touched down two hours earlier at La Guardia Airport. The air was fresh and crisp, and it felt more like an Idaho morning than September in the city. New York at its best. The smog had disappeared, and you could see everything for miles around. A day that would remind you how lucky you are to be alive. But all I felt at that moment was a dull sense of relief: we had made it to New York on time, and the ambulance was waiting for us on the tarmac.

We pulled up to the emergency room at NYU Medical Center in Lower Manhattan for our meeting with Dr. Kelly. Lee was taken straight to the neurosurgery ward by an attendant, and we were given directions to Dr. Kelly's office. Wendy and I hesitated, looking back at Lee as he was wheeled away in the opposite direction. He looked far younger than his thirty years.

Dr. Patrick Kelly, a stocky man with ruddy cheeks and a balding head, came around from behind his desk to shake hands with us. Wendy's brother Peter (also a physician) and Hank Harris, our family pediatrician and dear friend, were there, too. They had both come to New York on a day's notice to lend their support.

Dr. Kelly asked us how Lee had fared on the flight from Boise. "And what about you?" he added, peering over the glasses perched on his nose, his warmth and direct gaze reassuring.

I mumbled a reply, and he nodded. "It's toughest for the families," he said.

We handed him the MRIs we had brought from the hospital in Boise, and, within a few moments, he was explaining what he saw on the images. We understood some of what he said, and though much of it went over our heads, there was no mistaking that the diagnosis was bad—and I could see the gravity reflected in the faces of Peter and Hank as Dr. Kelly confirmed what we'd been told by the neurosurgeon in Boise.

"The tumor is extensive," Dr. Kelly said, his finger tracing the branching path of the shadow in Lee's brain. "And here," he pointed to the lower part of the image, "is where the fluid has been building up, where the base of the brain meets the spine. Lee needs surgery immediately to relieve the pressure. We'll also biopsy the tumor at the same time."

"How long has the tumor been there?" I asked.

"Alan," he said, "we have no way of knowing how the first cell got there, how long it's been dormant, or when it started multiplying. For all we know that one cell could have been there when Lee was born. If and when a cancer cell decides it wants to explode, that's what it'll do."

Dr. Kelly gestured to the chairs, inviting us all to sit down. His chief resident, he told us, would do the procedure. We already knew that Dr. Kelly had made plans for a weekend of sailing in Maine with his wife and friends. Lee, he assured us, would be in excellent hands, and it was not a difficult procedure. Dr. Kelly took his time with us, answering all of our questions. From his down-to-earth demeanor, you would have never guessed he was one of the most renowned neurosurgeons in the world. When Dr. Kelly spoke about Lee, we could see the compassion in his eyes. Lee was not just a faceless patient to him. We were not just another family on his list of morning meetings. Dr. Kelly, we were later told, treated everyone under his care this way.

"Here's my phone number," Kelly added. "If at any time during the weekend you have any concerns, please call me. I'll be back on Wednesday, and, in the meantime, my team will give me regular updates on how Lee is doing." He looked at his watch. "Lee should be out of surgery in a couple of hours."

We headed upstairs, and Wendy and I found ourselves once again in a hospital waiting room. We sat, we glanced at the clock on the wall, we paced, we sat, we talked a little, and we flipped through magazines whose words and pictures didn't register. We kept our emotions stowed away. I don't cry very often, and I don't remember if I did that day. But over the next six weeks, there would be times when the ground would fall away without warning and waves of grief overwhelmed me. Tears followed, uncontrollable. I never knew from one moment to the next what might trigger them—certain thoughts or words, hugging a close friend, special memories of Lee.

You do a lot of waiting in hospitals because there's not much else you can do. Patience takes on the proportions of a steep mountain face with no foothold in sight. Accepting that I was not in control was even harder, an unwelcome exercise in humility for someone who has always seen himself as self-reliant and in control. When it came to Lee, though, I'm not sure I had ever really been in control; I had just convinced myself that I was.

As you wait, you have a lot of time to think. You comb through the past in search of something you might have missed. If we had acted sooner on the signs of his illness—had the cancer been diagnosed earlier—would Lee have had a better chance? You think about your child as a toddler and as a kid and as a teen. Did you push him too hard or not enough? How did you handle his skinned knees and his successes? You remember the first time he got drunk. (Lee was 14 and had discovered the punchbowl at Heidi's Sweet Sixteen party.) You remember his first hockey goal.

Lee scored his first goal when he was on the Pee Wee hockey team at Roxbury Skate Club in Stamford. I was so thrilled that I framed the puck with the inscription *Lee's First Goal* and hung it in his room. I'm not sure now if I did it for Lee or for myself. I know it was what I wished my father had done for me. But was it what Lee needed? What if I had just savored that moment with my son, hugged him, and said, "Nice goal! I'm so proud of you." I don't remember if I did.

Then there was the tennis tournament. Lee was in high school, and I had asked him to be my partner; I wanted to show him I had confidence in him. We played against two of his friends, who were much better players than Lee. They kept hitting the balls to him and not to me, which pissed me off. Lee kept hitting the balls into the net. *For Christ's sake*, I screamed inside, *hit the god damn ball over the net!* Of course those words didn't come out of my mouth; they got lodged in my stomach. Lee was subdued as we walked off the court. I didn't know what to say to him. It was not the feel-good, father-son moment I had hoped for. I'd thought playing together might make Lee feel more confident, more included. Instead, I'd put him into a situation that made him feel the opposite.

I had high hopes that my son would be a superstar, a high achiever. I wanted that for all three of my kids. To me, Lee even looked the part: he was tall, good-looking, and physically strong.

"Lee was not a superstar," I confided to a friend when I was telling her about writing this book.

"You use that word a lot, Alan," she said.

I was taken aback. "Do I really?"

She reminded me that I had referred to the son of a family friend as a *superstar*; I spoke of the son of John Gunther (author of *Death Be Not Proud*) as a *superstar*; one of our board members, I told her, was a *superstar*. And so on.

"What does that mean, superstar? Is it important?" she asked.

When I thought about it later, I realized using the word was just a habit, old language that doesn't reflect how I think today. My knee-jerk admiration for *superstars* had a lot to do with the importance I used to place on "climbing the ladder," making money, winning, seeing one's name in lights. My friend had a point: The term is meaningless. And what does it imply about the people who (in my view) don't merit those accolades?

At my high school graduation, I was unabashedly proud to learn that I had won the Athlete-Scholar award of my class. It was an honor that

I admit still tickles me, a recognition for things I *did*. But awards don't reveal very much about who a person *is*, the kind of son, brother, father, husband, or friend you are. Whether you make the world a better place. Today, these things are far more meaningful to me. My greatest joy comes from seeing a smile on a boy's face as he leaves Lee Pesky Learning Center. From sensing the relief of parents who realize that their daughter with learning disabilities will be able to thrive, after all. I always wanted to be a person who leaves the world better than I found it. We raised our children that way, too—to stand up for and help those who are vulnerable and in need. I remember with pride when Greg was singled out in grade school for stepping in to protect a classmate who was being physically bullied.

But when our children were young, I also placed a great deal of importance on things that *don't* actually matter all that much. I took it for granted that "success," as measured by some unspecified standard, would make them happy and fulfilled. I also felt that their achievements would reflect well on me. And Lee, the most vulnerable of our three children, suffered as a result. I loved him as much as I loved Heidi and Greg, but in my old way of thinking, he did not have the makings of a superstar.

Lee's girlfriend, Criss, was recently asked to describe Lee and the qualities that had meant the most to her. Here's what she wrote:

> One snowy day, we cross-country skied into Alturas Lake; Lee was in front of me and at one point, he just turned around and smiled at me. He had the best smile . . . There are so many things I loved about Lee—his character, his personality, his smile, his sense of humor, his eyes, his smell. His smile always brightened my day. I just kept falling in love with him again and again. I was blessed with the greatest gift of all: his love and so many wonderful memories.

Her words were a gut punch. I grieved for the young man Criss described, the Lee I had never allowed myself to see. More than anything, I wish that Lee and I could have connected in a more open and tender way, with all defenses, expectations, and misunderstandings put aside. For much of our time together as father and son, we reacted to each other as two magnets

of like poles, never able to get very close. Today, I imagine how much fun
I would have had with my son had I seen *him*, rather than the son I hoped
he would be.

WENDY AND I spent most of that Labor Day weekend at the hospital, taking any time we were permitted to sit with Lee in the ICU. His head was
bandaged, and his 6'1" frame looked small and frail surrounded by the
jungle of tubes, machines, and monitors. He wasn't conscious, so all we
could do was hold his hand and talk to him, hoping he could hear us. The
rest of the time, Wendy and I walked and talked and walked some more.
We roamed all over Lower Manhattan to familiar spots, as if on autopilot.
We passed like sleepwalkers through the closely packed neighborhoods of
downtown. One minute we were in Chinatown, then we'd cross a street,
look up, and find ourselves in SoHo or Little Italy, as if stage sets had
suddenly switched on us.

That's how we happened upon the San Gennaro Festival in Little Italy
with its lighthearted throngs of people. We wandered through the crowds
and, by chance, were drawn to a stand surrounded by a cluster of people.
As we drew closer, we saw a young man seated at a table, his head bent in
concentration. He appeared to be doing the impossible: with a fine stick
pen under a magnifying glass, he was writing on a grain of rice. When he
finished, he picked up the minuscule work of art with a pair of tweezers
and placed it in a glass vial no more than a third of an inch long.

How many letters could he get on a grain of rice? I asked him, fascinated. Eight, including the spaces between words, he replied. Wendy
stepped forward and, with her shy smile, asked him if he would write *Love
Lee* on a grain of rice for her. A few minutes later, Wendy was clasping a
red cord dangling a small glass pendant that encased the words *Love Lee*
on a grain of rice. I hung it around her neck. Wendy only parted with the
pendant when she placed it with Lee at his funeral.

It's a strange sensation, carrying your grief around with you in a place
like New York City. You are never alone—traffic, crowds, and noise con-
stantly surround you. But you feel anonymous in your pain and discon-
nected from other people. Overlooked like a grain of rice. Yet you wonder

how anyone could *not* notice the pain that's written all over your face, the grief that seeps from your pores and through your fingertips.

ONCE LEE HAD recovered sufficiently from the surgery, he was moved from the ICU into his own room. Over the next few weeks, friends and family converged to be with him and to lend us support. They came with hugs, gifts, and memories of the times they had spent with Lee. People just showed up—even those we hadn't thought to contact. Perhaps they found it easier to be there, within a circle of support, rather than far away and wondering how Lee was doing and how they could help. Care packages, too, appeared out of nowhere. Coming home one night from the hospital, we found a box of homemade chocolate chip cookies at the door with a one-word note, "Hugs." We guessed it was from our friend Camilla, who several years earlier had arrived in New York as a solo transplant from Italy. She understood what it was to feel vulnerable. Little gestures like these were life preservers to us, and they reminded me of something my mother used to say that had always sounded like a cliché to me: *It's the thought that counts*. There, in the hospital, I understood. Kind words and thoughtful gestures are powerful medicine.

Heidi was with us at the hospital almost every day. Even though she was just shy of nine months pregnant and her home was a three-hour drive from the city, nothing seemed to stop her—the older sister who had bossed around the brother who had needled her mercilessly. She even registered for the birth at two different hospitals—NYU Medical Center and Yale New Haven Hospital—whichever would be closer when her time came. Heidi gave birth to her daughter, Eliza Lee, on September 18. Ten days later, Heidi returned to Lee's side.

Greg, meanwhile, was supposed to be starting grad school at the Tuck School of Business at Dartmouth. He went to New Hampshire for the start of the term, then abruptly returned to New York two days later. "I just need to be here," he told me. I nodded and hugged him. There was nothing more to say.

And Criss, as she had promised Lee, arrived in New York from Idaho just a few days after his surgery and stayed.

AT FIRST, OUR only concern was to get Lee the immediate care he needed. We couldn't think much further ahead than that. We were still hoping that Lee would somehow come through, that he could beat the cancer. *People do,* we told ourselves. But five days after Lee's surgery, Dr. Kelly shared the preliminary results of the biopsy with us, and it was terrible news. Lee had a glioblastoma.

A glioblastoma is the worst type of brain tumor one can have—an aggressive, fast-growing cancer whose malignant cells migrate quickly to adjacent brain tissue. It's difficult to treat and even harder to remove completely, as the growth tends to be diffuse, branching out to infiltrate other parts of the brain.[7] Glioblastomas are most often seen in middle-aged and older adults, but your chances of developing one are only about three in 100,000.[8] The odds are even lower for someone as young as Lee.

Eventually, the cancer would claim Lee's life. Only a very small percentage of patients survive beyond three years. Based on the information available at that point, Dr. Kelly couldn't tell us how much time Lee might have. He wanted to send the biopsy to a few other labs, including one in France for review by a renowned pathologist. Dr. Kelly knew the doctor well and had tremendous respect for her expertise. He wanted to have the best possible information before determining the next steps for Lee.

As we waited for the final pathology results, we continued to focus on Lee's recuperation from surgery. Every morning Lee would be bathed, and Criss or Greg would help him into a fresh hospital gown. Then it would be time for physical therapy. Lee's therapist was a delightful young woman with whom we instantly bonded. The routine usually involved Lee playing catch or kicking a big rubber ball while he was seated. On the rare days that he felt stronger, we would help support him while he tried to kick the ball standing up. It was like watching a toddler learn to kick a ball.

There were moments of optimism. Lee improved slightly after the pressure on his brain had been relieved, and the physical therapy also seemed to help him. He was awake and responsive at times, and he could eat and walk, albeit only with assistance. Although Lee still wasn't talking, he could communicate in other ways. Criss, who would crawl into Lee's hospital bed to hold him, was the most adept at interpreting his signals.

She could understand some of what he tried to communicate through mumbles and eye movements and by squeezing her hand. Even then, Lee's sense of humor never left him. With eye rolls and a lopsided grin, Lee joked about the awkwardness of personal hygiene in his debilitated state.

Lee had always been one to find humor in unlikely places. Criss told us a story about Lee that still makes her laugh. After a shower one day, before he got sick, Lee couldn't wait to tell Criss that he had discovered a new hair on his head. (He was, by then, virtually bald.) "You need to feel this. You need to see this!" he exclaimed with a big grin, proud of the one hair that had sprouted on the top of his head, coaxed out, perhaps, by the Rogaine he was using. Criss laughed and told him to stop using it. She loved him bald.

I couldn't tamp down my enthusiasm when I talked with Dr. Kelly about Lee's moments of improvement. But Dr. Kelly put his hand on my shoulder and gently explained that, yes, there would be moments of reprieve. "But it's like being on an elevator that's going down," he said. "Even though it may stop at a floor and remain there for a short period of time, it will continue going down."

Never before had I experienced such an excruciating feeling. Acceptance felt like surrender to me—a betrayal of Lee and my responsibility as a parent. I couldn't argue with the medical facts, but every cell in my body screamed resistance. Hope, in this case, was not my friend.

THE FIRST AND most important rule of parenthood is to keep your children safe.

I remember the clutch of fear as a new parent when Heidi had her first racking cough, and I realized just how vulnerable babies and toddlers are. It was up to us—to Wendy and me—to keep our young children alive and healthy until they could fend for themselves. It was the most important responsibility we would ever have. As our kids got older (and sturdier), my conception of "safe" morphed into something broader and less clearly defined. Protecting our children became more about preparing them, giving them the tools they'd need in life to be healthy and happy, to thrive and be self-reliant. And Lee, due to his learning disabilities, needed more of our intervention than Heidi or Greg.

Much of the time, we were flailing. There was no one we could call on to help Lee in a meaningful and sustainable way, no credible resources we could rely on. And because so much of one's early life is about learning, I came to equate Lee's ability to thrive—even to survive—with his ability to get through school. His path was bumpy and fraught, punctuated with promising starts, then more stumbles. We encouraged him, coaxed him, supported him, pushed him, watched him fall, and saved him. The help and protection I gave Lee often took the form of last-minute—and, to my mind, urgent and necessary—rescues, especially when Lee was in high school and college, when the academic consequences of falling behind could be severe.

When Lee was accepted to Lafayette College, he was thrilled. But Lafayette, like most schools at the time, offered no accommodations for students with learning disabilities, even though it had been seven years since the Individuals with Disabilities Education Act had become law. Universities and colleges still largely viewed learning disabilities as the student's problem to deal with on her or his own. School had always been hard for Lee, and college was even harder. With his auditory processing challenges and labored, often illegible, handwriting, Lee struggled in freshman classes; many of them were lecture-based and required tons of reading and scrupulous notetaking by the students—a teaching approach not designed for kids with learning disabilities.

One aspect of freshman life, however, was easy for Lee: making new friends and socializing. Partying with friends became an escape for him. The more frustrated with school Lee became, the more he partied, but the more he partied, the harder school got. He was devastated when he realized at the end of freshman year that he was flunking out and wouldn't be invited to return. And I was equally disappointed.

I decided to intercede on Lee's behalf—this time, to plead his case with the college. I knew that Lee was doing the best he could under the circumstances. The school had no knowledge of his learning issues (not unusual in the early '80s), and I believed his challenges should be taken into consideration for a second chance. At the time, I was a trustee of Lafayette College, and I'm somewhat embarrassed now to admit that I had absolutely no compunction about trying to beg a meeting with the academic dean through my contacts at the school.

The dean was hesitant but agreed to meet with me. I explained the challenges presented by Lee's learning differences—that it was not a matter of inadequate motivation or capacity. Many learning tasks simply took Lee longer to complete because of how his brain processed information. I asked them to consider giving Lee another chance. The Dean eventually agreed, but he told me that Lee would have to go to summer school. Only if Lee was able to pull off Bs or better in all three of his summer classes would he be allowed to return on academic probation for his sophomore year. Fair enough. Lee and I both knew it would be tough for him, but he was determined to give it a shot.

In the summer, distractions on campus were minimal, and Lee seemed to tap into inner resources that, perhaps, he never knew he had. He focused, studied hard, and finished summer school with two As and a B. Lee would be allowed to return to school in the fall. The college made no further accommodations for him for the rest of his time there, and he graduated in four years. Not with stellar grades, but he did it.

I was impressed to the point of tears. Because his brain was wired differently, Lee had to climb a mountain that most other kids don't have to. Kids with learning disabilities—even those who have had the benefit of effective academic intervention—have to work twice as hard as others to achieve similar results. But there's a silver lining: students who are given the opportunity and the tools to address their learning challenges often develop remarkable determination and resilience, traits we often observe in kids at Lee Pesky Learning Center.

Who knows if Lee would have ultimately been better off had I not intervened to negotiate a second chance for him at college. Perhaps he would have figured things out for himself and been the better for it. Greg once said to me, "Lee's journey *was* very different, but he was going to get to where he needed to be. It might have taken him longer, there may have been more skinned knees, but he would have gotten there."

How did Lee feel about being bailed out by his father? We never talked about it, but he seemed relieved and grateful that he was able to complete college. At the same time, I wouldn't be surprised if Lee was also uncomfortable about the fact that I had intervened. Gratitude and resentment can go hand in hand. Had I been in Lee's shoes, I would have been torn: Hitting my goals is extremely important to me, but I'd much rather do it on my own.

Would I still take the same approach today—coming to the rescue, say, of a grandchild—that I took with Lee? Probably. But it's a messy choice, rife with conflicts. On the one hand, I want to see my loved ones realize their dreams. On the other hand, I wouldn't want their confidence and satisfaction to be tainted by my intervention. Moreover, I have come to recognize that I *benefited* from my father's lack of involvement in my choices when I was young. His approach allowed me to become who I am by getting there on my own. Finally, there is the uncomfortable truth that privilege played a big part in our ability to rescue Lee in ways that wouldn't be possible for many parents.

Yet when all is said and done, I would never have *not* done what I did to help Lee. And I would do it again, though I hope I would do so with a greater sense of awareness of all the factors at play. I think Greg was probably right about some of my efforts on Lee's behalf. Even if I hadn't intervened, maybe things would somehow have worked out in the end.

But when Lee was thirty years old, and he needed help the most, there was nothing I could do to save him.

ONE MORNING AT the end of September, we got a phone call from Dr. Kelly. Could we meet that evening at 5? He had the final pathology results.

It was about 6:30 when he finally walked into the empty waiting room, now dimly lit. The hospital had a deserted feel to it, the halls quiet. Dr. Kelly looked haggard and was still wearing his blue-green scrubs, which were splattered with blood from his last surgery.

"I want to apologize for being so late. I needed a few minutes alone before I saw you."

Wendy and I stood up.

"The results came back from the lab in France and have confirmed what I was afraid of: there's nothing we can do to save Lee's life."

He put his arms around us, and he cried with us, this tough man who had a light touch and an enormous heart. I don't remember anything more about that night. When you hear those words, nothing else matters. There is no space for anything else.

Chapter 5

A Vulnerable Rebel

"There's a bump on your prostate, Alan, and your PSA levels are elevated," the urologist said. "You need to get a biopsy. I've made an appointment for you tomorrow at St. Luke's Prostate Cancer Detection Center in Boise."

My mouth went dry. I thought, *Who goes to a cancer center if they don't have cancer?* I swallowed. "Could it really be cancer?" I asked.

"We won't know until they have the biopsy results," he said.

I had been hoping for a "Probably not," or a "Don't worry, it's just a precaution."

I was 56 years old, and it was four years before Lee got sick. I was scared, more than I had ever been in my life. Lonely, too. Wendy and Heidi were traveling in Europe with Wendy's parents. Greg was doing a summer internship in New York. I drove home from Boise after the procedure, convinced I had prostate cancer. It was Friday night, and I was not looking forward to spending the weekend alone with my terrifying thoughts. I called Lee.

Lee had moved to Ketchum a few months earlier after having quit a junior management position with an international construction company in New York. I had thought the job would be great for him. He hated it. Ketchum, Idaho, population 2,500, was where he wanted to be. He had come through a period in his life dominated by academics, school sports, and, more recently, a rigid corporate environment—areas in which he had struggled. Here in Idaho, he could just *be*. He could work and do the things he loved: hiking, biking, camping, skiing, and playing golf.

"Would you have dinner with me tonight?" I asked him. I really needed to talk.

"Sure," he said easily.

Over dinner, I told him my news. He was the first one in the family to hear it. He didn't hug me or tell me not to worry, but I saw love and concern in his eyes. His presence was comforting. Lee was a good listener. He didn't press you or pepper you with questions. I wish I could remember what he said, but I do know his words, though few, were just right, enough. In one of my most vulnerable moments, I needed Lee, and he was there for me.

As it turned out, I didn't have cancer. But in a way, I'm grateful I had the cancer scare and that Wendy, Heidi, and Greg weren't there. And I'm grateful that Lee was. It is one of my most precious memories of Lee. It was the closest we had ever been.

Now our son was going to die. There was nothing we or the medical community could do about it. A glioblastoma is not contained. It has no clear boundaries. It resembles a galaxy of stars radiating throughout the brain. Surgically removing the entire tumor is impossible. And chemotherapy or radiation would be risky, we were told. All that coursing poison sent to attack the tumor could damage other parts of the brain.

We were asked by the team caring for Lee if we would consider allowing him to receive an experimental treatment as part of a broader study that might benefit future glioblastoma patients. It was unlikely to make a difference for Lee, though. After the radiologist had finished explaining the nature of the study and the radiation and chemo it would entail, we met with Dr. Kelly.

"If Lee were your son, what would you do?" I asked him.

He didn't respond right away. He closed his eyes and took a deep breath. "The information that will be gathered in this clinical trial may help us with future cancer patients. But I can't tell you that it will help Lee. What you see now with Lee is the best he'll be. If we start doing the experimental protocol, we'll be doing things to Lee's brain that we can't possibly predict or fully understand. He can't walk on his own anymore. He doesn't talk. And his condition will continue to worsen." Because it was an experimental treatment, Dr. Kelly couldn't rule out the possibility that it might buy Lee a little more time. But it wouldn't save him. And the quality of Lee's life would continue to deteriorate.

Our instinct was to say no. But it was still an excruciating decision. Should we give our approval for Lee to be included in a clinical trial that *might* help others in the distant future? For a treatment that *might* extend his life but would likely increase his discomfort and perhaps cause him greater suffering? How does one do such a calculation? We knew Lee could not understand the choice before him. He was unable to communicate his wishes. How could we know what was right for him? Wendy and I were left to make this decision about the life of our child, a decision no parent is equipped to make, a decision that cannot be undone. Even today, I have trouble writing or talking about it.

We decided not to proceed with the experimental protocol. It might make us feel slightly better for a moment, if only for having done *something*. But we refused to put Lee through that. I'm grateful that Wendy and I were of one mind. Having a disagreement about something so important at such a grievous time would have been unbearable. Once we made the decision, we never doubted it was the right thing for Lee. But there was no redemption or comfort in making it.

It was just a matter of time, then. There was nothing we could do other than try to make Lee as comfortable as possible for this last period of his life, having no clear idea how long that might be. Today, about 25 percent of people with glioblastomas survive between three to five years after diagnosis. For Senators Edward Kennedy and John McCain, it was about a year; for Beau Biden, nearly two years. We were told that Lee probably wouldn't have that much time. His tumor was enormous, and it had not been caught early. But we had no way of knowing then how short his time would be—only 2½ months after the tumor was discovered.

We all pulled closer together, creating a loving and protective circle around Lee and a life raft of sorts for ourselves. Over those remaining weeks, time was suspended. There was rarely a day that Wendy, Heidi, Greg, Criss, Bernice (Wendy's mother), and I weren't together for eight, sometimes twelve, hours a day. We always stayed at the hospital until 8 p.m. and then either stopped somewhere for dinner or picked up food on Third Avenue and ate it in the car on our way home. By midnight, I was exhausted, but I didn't want to fall asleep because I knew the next day could be worse. I couldn't help wondering about Lee's level of awareness and what he was thinking. I couldn't stop wondering if he was afraid. Our hearts wrenched at not knowing whether we were able to comfort him. Most days, he did not seem to know us.

There's no way to get around the slow agony of loss. There are no shortcuts or bypasses. Love and friendships are what pulled us through the tunnel. Wendy and I are blessed with an extraordinary bond. There was never one moment of anger or a word of recrimination between us those two and a half months when Lee was sick and dying. It was the unwavering, unconditional love and acceptance of my wife and children that largely kept me sane. I know it was the same for Wendy.

My only self-medication while Lee was in the hospital was walking. Our apartment and my office were about thirty blocks away from NYU Medical Center, which is on 32nd Street and First Avenue. Every day, I would walk the two miles or so to the hospital and then back the same distance. Most days I made the trip twice; some days, three times. I tried to vary the route, but some streets got more wear and tear from me than others. Over time, I came to know every crack in the pavement, each food vendor along the way, and the window displays of every storefront. Only the people I passed every day changed. Most were dressed in light, breezy clothing as they enjoyed the unusually mild fall weather, a jarring contrast with the depressing, clinical world of the hospital.

There were times when my thoughts would turn dark, veering into an angry and resentful conversation with God. I railed at him, the god I didn't believe in, while I walked those streets. "Really?" I raged in my helplessness. "You could have taken any one of these people, and you chose Lee? What about that person over there? He obviously hasn't taken very good care of himself. And what about the guy I just passed who was smoking up a storm?"

I had appointed myself the judge of strangers, a stand-in for God. They were horrible thoughts.

WHEN LEE GOT sick, he was just entering the sweetest moment in his life. Everything seemed to be falling into place for him. The fact that Lee had met someone whom he cared about deeply and who brought him joy in the last years of his life was the greatest gift imaginable. And it gave us a measure of comfort, however slim, as we faced the random cruelty of it all. Criss loved Lee for who he was, which gave him a sense of confidence and acceptance that he perhaps didn't find among us, his immediate family. And he was able to share the things he loved with the woman he loved.

In Idaho, Lee's creativity had space to flourish and manifest. He and a high school friend, Austin Stewart, brainstormed an idea for a business—and it was a winner: "The Buckin' Bagel: *The Eastern Bagel with the Western Kick.*" They started with a small shop in Ketchum. To my mind, it served the best bagels anywhere, including New York. Austin handled the business side, and Lee was the creative guy who invented the recipes and menus and took charge of the decor. Lee had style, and it showed in the café, which had an irresistible personality and vibe. People enjoyed hanging out at the Buckin' Bagel, with its cowboy-western-New-York kitsch. Like Lee, the place was fun.

Above all, Lee loved it. Working in an office was never going to be his thing, but he thrived on having his own business, even though it meant getting up every day at 4 a.m. to make fresh bagels for the day. Lee obsessed over the quality of the product and was reluctant to expand the business until they got the formula just right. Their signature bagel was called the Power Bagel, and it was filled with all sorts of good stuff—perfect fuel for a hike, bike, or ski. After a couple of years, the Buckin' Bagel opened two stores in Boise, with plans for additional locations elsewhere in the state.

The business closed a year after Lee's death. Austin decided he didn't want to continue with it on his own. But I'm happy that Lee had seen it become a place that mattered to the community, where people were happy to be. Lee had ideas that got people's attention and captured their imagination. He was the youngest entrepreneur in a family of entrepreneurs. Something I had never expected.

I was seeing sides of Lee in those last few years before he got sick that I'd never seen before. I'll never forget Heidi and Rick's wedding. Lee stood at the rehearsal dinner and gave one of the funniest impromptu speeches I'd ever heard at a wedding. Totally off the cuff, Lee talked about his sister, with whom his relationship had improved markedly from the days of the Kane Lake episode. Lee had everyone in the room in the palm of his hand. I'd never seen my son do anything like that before. Perhaps I didn't know him very well.

Greg has reminded me that Lee was always an out-of-the-box thinker. He was far more inclined to take risks than Greg or Heidi. As a kid, Greg was often perturbed by his big brother's rebellious nature. But he also admired the boldness and wit of Lee's exploits.

One such episode involved a Porsche. Both Lee and Heidi had their driver's licenses by then, and my company car, a sleek black Targa, was strictly off limits. *Verboten.* So, of course, it was irresistible to Lee, who took the Porsche out for a drive when Wendy and I were out of town for a week. To give me an extra poke in the eye, Lee smoked a couple of cigarettes and left the butts and some matches in the car. It would have never even occurred to Heidi or Greg to do something like that. "Not in a million years," Greg said. He still grins whenever he tells the story.

And it didn't occur to me that any of my kids would do that—not even Lee. So, when I got in the car shortly after we returned from vacation and I saw the cigarettes, I assumed they'd been left behind by the mechanic who had done my last car service. I was annoyed but didn't give it another thought. A few years after Lee died, Greg confessed on behalf of his brother. "Remember those cigarettes you found in your Porsche, Dad? Well, guess what."

I had to laugh. Lee was probably disappointed that I didn't catch on at the time, that I missed the "calling card" he left behind. Because, when you think about it, adventures are way more fun when other people can admire your exploits and appreciate your moxie. Although the nature of our adventures was different, Lee and I had that trait in common. "I think

Alan's adventures are great, but why does he have to brag about them?" our friend Camilla asks, her European sensibilities put off by my eagerness to share, while her husband, Stuart (my confidante and walking buddy), smiles and says not a word.

As Lee explored his wild side, he displayed his creative flair and entrepreneurial spirit. Our house in Connecticut came with a wonderful old greenhouse kitted out with a furnace, sink, and retractable windows—the works. There were no green thumbs in our family, so this temple to horticulture was completely wasted on us. Or so we thought.

One late summer morning, Frank, the handyman who came to help us on weekends with landscaping and fixer-upper tasks, pulled me aside with an odd expression on his face. It looked like he was trying not to laugh.

"Alan, there's something I've got to talk to you about."

"Sure, Frank. What's up?"

"There's some stuff growing in the greenhouse. I think you should see it."

When I sat Lee down an hour or so later to have a talk with him, there were several emotions dueling in me. This was the 1980s, and drug offenses were taken very seriously. "Are you kidding me?" I shouted at Lee. "You may want to go to jail for growing pot, but I have no interest in joining you!" At the same time, part of me grudgingly admired Lee's ingenuity and chutzpah.

Today, I love the fact that he grew pot in our greenhouse. It makes me smile. I love Lee for the spirit he had and that he was willing to show it.

Lee could be very funny. He could convey more in a few words than most people can in full sentences. His humor was quirky and dry, never mean or sarcastic. In his senior year of high school, Lee went with a group of his friends to a school dance. The details about the event have long since escaped my memory, but what I do remember with laser-like clarity is the phone call we received the following morning from the mother of one of Lee's friends. I'll call the girl "Ellen."

"This is Nancy, Ellen's mom. Sorry to bother you, but did Lee come home from the dance last night?"

"Yeah," I said. "He's in his room, probably still asleep."

"Would you mind asking him if he saw Ellen when he was leaving, or if he knows where she is?"

"Sure, no problem. I'll call you back in a few minutes."

I ran upstairs and quietly opened Lee's door. The shades were still down, and the room was dim. Looking closely, I noticed a tousled head of blonde hair peeping out of the covers next to Lee's dark head.

"For Christ's sake!" I yelled. I slammed the door and ran back downstairs, feeling a bit like I was in a sitcom. I picked up the phone.

"Nancy? It's Alan. Everything's okay. Your daughter came over to the house last night. She's here. She's fine." I hung up as quickly as I could without seeming rude, then ran back upstairs and politely told Ellen we would be happy to take her home as soon as possible.

The next day, Lee stopped by Wendy's office in the city to speak with her about something.

"Why on Earth did you do that last night?" she asked.

"I just wanted to show you I wasn't gay," he said with a straight face and a shrug.

LEE'S COUSIN MARK, his periodic partner-in-crime and close friend, described Lee well: "Lee was the black sheep in his family, but I think he turned that energy into something that was kind of irrepressibly charismatic. He was just fun to be around. You wanted to be with Lee."

We heard similar thoughts from so many of Lee's friends. They loved being with him.

So his friends came to be with Lee in his last weeks. They came from all over: California; North Carolina; Washington, DC; Connecticut; Idaho; and Vancouver, BC. It was astonishing how the news had spread. Friends called and they wrote. They were wonderful as they sat with Lee; they kidded with him, pushed his wheelchair around, and even fed him.

I was profoundly moved and awed by their tenderness and cheerfulness. Are they insulated by their youth, I wondered? Do they have a different relationship to death from that of their elders, like us? How do they do it?

It was rare that Lee could even give his visitors a response, but sometimes we were surprised. I remember a visit from Wendy's brother Michael. He had come from work and was wearing a particularly beautiful tie. Lee seemed pleased to see his uncle, but his eyes really lit up when he noticed the tie, and he pointed weakly at it.

"Do you like the tie, Lee?" Michael asked. He knew how much Lee liked nice clothing.

Lee didn't respond, but Michael undid his tie and draped it around Lee's neck.

Lee recognized some of his friends, others he didn't. Some he knew on one visit, but not on the next. They reminisced about the times they'd had with him and told Lee about the fun things they planned to do with him once he got better—all the time knowing it wouldn't happen. Listening, though, we believed they meant everything they said, and I hope Lee did, too.

It was a beautiful thing to see, but impossibly difficult for us to witness. One of Lee's friends spent four hours with him, pushing Lee in his wheelchair through the hospital gardens and then sitting by his bedside, just talking. When he left Lee's room and said good-bye to us, he sobbed, knowing he would never see Lee again. I was overwhelmed and grateful for the love and the warmth his friends showed Lee, but, oh, how I cried when I saw them with him, knowing that Lee should be as vibrant and healthy as they.

Looking back now, I still can't comprehend how we survived the loss of our son and the eternity of watching him die. We lived a lifetime in 69 days that passed far too quickly. A grief that deep should kill you, but it doesn't. You're in another world, but somehow still in the awfulness of the reality. Wendy has said, "That's when friends and family really became so important. The strength of the people who came to be with us just kept us going." What saved us was absorbing the pain together as a family body.

I'M GRATEFUL THAT my relationship with Lee improved in the last years of his life, after he had moved to Ketchum. Lee was happy and seemed to be at ease with himself. I was more accepting of who he was, seeing sides of him that I had never seen before. I watched as Lee actualized *his* picture of well-being and fulfillment by following his own path rather than mine. He had chosen a different kind of life for himself from the one I had at his age, or from the ones Heidi and Greg had, and I could see that it worked for him.

For a long time, it was easy for me to attribute the rift in our relationship to Lee's learning disabilities and the frustrations he experienced as a result of those challenges. The more I learned about learning disabilities, the more I'd think, "If only I'd known. I would have been more supportive. We could have helped Lee in a far more constructive way." And this is true. There's no doubt that I would have handled things differently had I known what I know today. And there's no doubt that it would have had a significant and positive impact on Lee and our relationship.

But that's too easy, a comfortable way for me to gloss over my role in our relationship. The fact is, I was a tough father for Lee to have. He didn't need to be a clone of me, but I wanted our eldest son to be accomplished in some fashion. I wanted him to do something that would set him apart, that one could point to as admirable, not just average. Something I could talk about with pride. We were told by the neurologist when Lee was a kid that he would always be constrained by issues that were not his fault. But I resisted the idea that there was *nothing* Lee could do about it.

It's easy for us as parents to place the weight of our expectations on our children. I did so with all three of my kids. *I know best. Trust me. This worked for me, so it will work for you.* Wendy often reminds me that my way is not always the right way. This is one of my greatest challenges. I'm getting better, but I still fight it. It's one thing to set foundational expectations for your children—honesty, hard work, kindness, courtesy, and respect. Best done, as my father did, by example. But it's another thing to start mapping out their lives for them. As if you don't trust them to do it for themselves.

I can only imagine how hard it must have been for Lee to try to please me. How he must have ached that he just couldn't do it. Because I was hoping that he would become someone he couldn't be. Someone he didn't even *want* to be. This was apparently on Lee's mind after he got sick.

While he was still in the hospital in Boise, a day or so after the tumor was discovered, Lee asked Criss about her father's relationship with her brother: Was her father—an attorney—okay with the fact that her brother had chosen to become a chef? In other words, was he disappointed in his son?

It must have been one of the last conversations Criss had with Lee, as his ability to communicate declined precipitously before we even got him to New York. "Lee knew he couldn't live up to Alan's expectations," Criss later shared. "Lee was different; he wanted to live life his way, and he did. Lee was in a very good place in his life before he died. He had a lot of great things happening, and he was really happy before he got sick."

A few years ago, I read Ron Fournier's moving book, *Love That Boy*, about his experience parenting a son with Asperger's. He observes that we sometimes lose our way as parents: we want our kids to be happy, and then we tell them how to do it—not realizing that our aspirations for our children are not necessarily theirs. We have two kids, he concludes: the one we hoped for, and the one we've got. Which one, he asks, are you going to treasure?

Fournier had a conversation with his son Tyler that I wish I could have had with Lee.

"You have a picture in your head of what makes a kid happy," Tyler tells his father. "But then you have a kid and it doesn't turn out that way. That just means your picture didn't come true. It doesn't mean I'm not happy. I have a different picture." Both father and son then acknowledge that neither of them is happy all the time in the picture they have created for themselves.[9]

LEE SPENT THE last few weeks of his life at our house in Connecticut, where he had grown up, ridden his dirt bike in the backyard, skated on the frozen pond in the winter, hung out with his friends, and grown pot in the greenhouse.

The last photo we have of Lee was taken about a week before he died. Whenever we could, we'd bring him out onto the terrace overlooking the garden so he could feel the sun on his face and see the colors of the leaves. That day, Lee is bundled in a blanket and wearing a Buckin' Bagel baseball cap. On his lap is baby Eliza Lee, his niece, who had just come into the world six weeks earlier. There is a small smile on Lee's face, but his eyes are blank, as if he's already gone.

Lee died on November 6th, three weeks after we moved him home, sixty-nine days after he was diagnosed. Lee was surrounded by the people who loved him when he left.

There isn't a day that goes by that I don't think of Lee.

Chapter 6

What I Cannot Know

If you stand with your toes in the Atlantic on 'Sconset Beach on Nantucket Island, you will be among the first people in the country to see the sunrise. Wendy and I have been going there since the 1980s, nearly every year for a week in November. Only a few thousand hardy year-round residents remain on the island during the bleak winter months, when the island is a very different place from the popular resort whose summer population pushes 50,000. In November, town is empty. Many stores and restaurants are shuttered for the winter, and the beaches are blustery and deserted. This is when the island most feels like the isolated outpost it is—30 miles from the coast of Massachusetts on the one side, 3,200 miles of ocean stretching to the next continent on the other side. We love it. It is our time to get away from the world and to be alone with each other and our thoughts. After Lee died, our days on the island took on a special meaning.

We plan our visit around the anniversary of Lee's death. Wendy and I make it a point to start and end that day with a walk from Quidnet to 'Sconset beach. We rarely see another person. A couple of years after Lee died, we were on our ritual November 6th beach walk, when a seal popped its head out of the ocean and looked our way. We thought nothing of it and continued walking. A few minutes later, there he was again, his head bobbing over the waves. Wendy stopped this time. Was it the same seal? The seal disappeared again. We walked on, scanning the waves more often now. When we were ready to leave the beach and head home, we looked out to the ocean one last time, and to our surprise, the seal now appeared close to the beach. So close, we could see his brown eyes and the gleam of his coat. Wendy and the seal looked at each other. Then he was gone.

"That was so strange," she said. "Was it some sort of sign? Do you think it might be . . . ?"

I smiled and hugged Wendy and tried to make light of it. "It's just a coincidence. But a nice one."

Since then, we have seen a seal—sometimes many seals—nearly every year on our November 6th beach walk. Some years, a seal bobs near us and dives down, then comes up, dives, and resurfaces, again and again. Other years, a few seals seem to tag along with us on our walk. We look for our seals—*the* seal—every year, and when we see him, Wendy stops and grabs my hand.

Wendy tried to explain it once to a friend: "It was a definite thing—not a coincidence. There was a presence that first time. And every time since then. I remember it vividly."

"Don't you think so, Alan?" she asked me. "Couldn't it be?"

It could be. I don't know. But it's meaningful.

"We all look for signs, don't we?" Wendy said.

So many people reached out to us after Lee passed away. I don't remember everyone who did, but I remember those who didn't. A few people wrote notes about faith and religion. "We hope you've been able to find comfort in your faith," they'd say, or something to that effect. We have friends whose deep faith and belief in God have brought them tremendous comfort in difficult times, so I understand why they wrote what they did. But for me, their words about God didn't register. The rabbi who spoke at Lee's funeral began his remarks with these words: "You might be asking yourselves how there could be a God who would allow this beautiful young man to be taken away in the prime of his life."

"What does God have to do with it?" I thought.

Everyone wants to give solace, and many of us have no idea how to go about it. I say this as one who has grieved and as one who has witnessed the shattering grief of others. Watching the devastation unfolding on someone's face is hard. It's uncomfortable. Sometimes avoidance is easier. About a week after Lee's funeral, Wendy came home from Atkinson's, our local supermarket, and told me that as she headed down one of the aisles, she noticed a friend at the far end. When the man spotted her, he turned and went the other way.

She was more puzzled than upset by it. "Maybe you should wear a sign around your neck that says, 'Just give me a hug. I promise not to bite,'" I joked. I, too, had experienced awkward silences, had noticed averted eyes when I was at the gym or post office or just walking around town. It's not that those friends didn't care—they probably just didn't know what to say.

At times, I didn't know how to sit in the presence of my own grief or how to act around others. I was angry, raw. The niceties were gone, my guardrails dismantled. I remember one encounter, a few months after Lee's death. I was walking in Manhattan and happened to run into a college acquaintance. It was near the corner of 55th and Fifth, where the old Gotham Hotel used to be, where my partners and I had launched our advertising agency thirty years before. It was early morning, and the street was quiet.

I was so wrapped up in my thoughts that I didn't notice the man until he was in front of me.

"Alan! Hi," he said and clapped me on the shoulder. "So sorry. I heard about your son."

At first I didn't recognize him. Then I remembered him from school. A guy I had never really liked. "Thanks, Ed," I muttered, just wanting to move on.

As I turned to go, he said, "Yeah, well, I guess bad things happen to all of us."

I stopped and looked at him. "Go fuck yourself," I said and walked away.

What I have learned about grieving and being around friends who have lost loved ones is that although you can't fix it or make it better, you *can* offer comfort. Look them in the eyes and take their hand. "I'm thinking of you" is all you need to say. Or don't say anything. A hug can say it all. But don't look away.

I am Jewish, but I'm not religious. We go to services occasionally, usually once a year on High Holy Days, but that's about it. Our children were brought up with this casual approach to the Jewish faith. Our son Greg has chosen to raise his children in a more observant way; Heidi has no connection to religion at all. I respect the choices both our children have made. For me, the question of whether I am "a believer" is beside the point. What matters is how I respond to suffering, how I *act* on my beliefs. The values I strive to live by—though I don't always succeed—are not religiously based, yet they derive from something bigger than I. From something more than my immediate needs or concerns, or those of my family.

As my family and friends can tell you, I take strong positions on a range of humanitarian issues, and I am not afraid to share my opinions. But I don't want to be a flamethrower from the sidelines. (Few things aggravate me more than listening to people who gripe, yet seem unwilling to do something about whatever it is they are complaining about.) It's incumbent on me to take part in finding solutions for the things that matter most to me. And when I participate, I feel less helpless. I feel good.

In 1975, when I was still at the agency I founded with my partners, I was approached about helping with advertising to support The Coalition to Free Soviet Jews. I was asked because I'm Jewish. But I chose to act because I wanted to help those who were being persecuted for their beliefs—Jews, some of whom had escaped the Holocaust only thirty years earlier. How is it possible, I wondered, for the world to forget so quickly?

Fast-forward another 30 years. Women, men, and children were being slaughtered in Darfur solely because of the tribes they belonged to. Wendy and I initiated and helped underwrite a four-day event in our community to promote awareness and raise funds for the genocide survivors. More recently, I have been appalled by the vilification of our immigrant communities of color. I was disgusted by the deliberately cruel separation of families carried out by the previous administration, the effects of which were felt in communities around the country, including our own. Wendy and I are staunch supporters of a volunteer-based alliance in Idaho that provides assistance, advocacy, and comfort to immigrant families at risk—people who are our friends and neighbors.

Parents taken away from their children. Husbands separated from wives. Families needlessly torn apart. For me, such tragedies cut close to home. Learning disabilities can wreak havoc on individuals, but they can also devastate families—through divorce, joblessness, and, in extreme cases, suicide. The Lee Pesky Learning Center (LPLC) was my response to this suffering, much of it as invisible as the disability that causes it. Founding LPLC was also my response to the helplessness I felt with Lee.

I'm a brainstormer, instigator, organizer, and galvanizer. And I'm stubborn. When I make a commitment to help address an issue or solve a problem, and the solution is not apparent, I'll keep at it until I figure it out—as I did with Lee Pesky Learning Center. Financial security has made it easier for me to act on my desires to help. My greatest admiration is reserved for those doing heart-wrenching work every day. Those who eschew their own physical comfort, safety, and financial security to serve others, be it on the frontlines of humanitarian assistance, in education, or in addressing poverty and racism. I am in awe of the countless volunteers and aid workers who have dedicated themselves to refugees from the Middle East and Africa, of nuns who minister to the indigenous populations of the Amazon, of teachers who work for a pittance in our most underfunded school districts and spend their own money to buy textbooks and school supplies for their students. And, more recently, I think of the healthcare professionals around the world who sacrificed themselves to care for the sick and dying during the COVID-19 pandemic.

There are so many courageous individuals who do the impossible every day. Ordinary people making an extraordinary difference. If there is a God, this is where I see his presence.

SINCE LEE BECAME ill and died, I have become less absolute in my thinking and more open to things I can't explain. Like the signs Wendy speaks of, like the appearance of a seal on a beach. After Lee died, Criss told us about a hike she took with Tanner, Lee's dog, to a mountain lake she and Lee often visited together. As Criss and Tanner crested the trail and arrived at the lake, Criss heard a sound and looked up. Flying low, directly above them, was an eagle. She believed it was Lee, and I understood.

In 1995, when Lee was in the hospital in New York, Yom Kippur fell on October 4th. It is the one religious holiday that Wendy and I try to observe every year. Yom Kippur is considered the holiest day in the Jewish calendar—the Day of Atonement, on which we are meant to fast, pray, and make amends for our sins. The ritual also includes a prayer for the deceased, and Wendy and I go to services to pay our respects to our parents. We didn't want to leave Lee on Yom Kippur. We had spent every day with him since he was diagnosed with the brain tumor. Yet it seemed more important than ever for us to observe the holiday. Wendy and I wanted to do it with Lee, in the sanctuary of his hospital room. I turned to an old friend for help. I asked Elaine Harris, who is very observant in her faith, if she could condense the day-long Yom Kippur service into an hour that would capture the spirit of the day.

Following Elaine's distilled version, I performed the service at Lee's bedside while Wendy held his hand. I spoke the words I usually hear a rabbi reciting, calling for self-reflection, atonement, forgiveness, and thoughts for loved ones who have died. I'd heard these passages dozens of times in my life but had never *felt* them. But here with Lee, his head covered in white gauze instead of a yarmulke, the prayers carried a weight and clarity I'd never experienced. In that moment, we were living the meaning of Yom Kippur. That sacred ritual hour brought us a measure of peace and solace in our devastation. Lee was awake, but he gave no sign of recognition. I hope, somehow, the service gave him comfort.

A CAB DROPPED us off at the address we had been given in the Flatbush section of Brooklyn. It was a busy street of modest homes and a couple of mom-and-pop kosher convenience stores. Wendy and I climbed the three steps, then paused to look at each other. "Let's just see what he has to say," I said.

Wendy pushed the doorbell. An accented voice asked for our names, instructed us to wait in the hallway, then buzzed us in. After the door closed behind us and our eyes adjusted to the dim lights, we found ourselves looking into a room cluttered with heavy furniture and tasseled lamps with colored shades. The dark red carpet sucked up whatever light could filter through the heavily curtained windows. Intricate tapestries and scrolls covered most of the walls. The room was musty, and incense hung in the air.

Wendy squeezed my arm and pointed to shelves along the far wall. They were lined with jars of different shapes and sizes filled with twisted roots and withered herbs, some floating in yellowish liquids. A few jars contained disturbing shapes that looked like they might have tails and other appendages. Things that shouldn't be in jars in a house in Brooklyn. I wanted to leave, but Wendy kept an iron grip on my arm. We had come to see a faith healer.

It had been five days since Dr. Kelly told us that nothing could be done to save Lee's life. Around the same time, Wendy heard from her sister-in-law, Margie, about a friend, Howard, who had been cured by a rabbinical spiritual healer. Howard had been terminally ill with HIV. As a last resort, he was referred to a rabbi—a Kaballah mystic—who had emigrated from Morocco and now lived in Brooklyn. In a series of visits, the rabbi—I'll call him Ephraim—had cured Howard. We spoke with Howard by phone, and he confirmed everything that Margie had told Wendy: his illness was in remission, he felt great, and he had every hope of living a long life.

We knew nothing about Kabbalah, a mystical branch of Judaism. If you were to give me an exam on it, I'd have to leave most of the questions blank. Adherents, I'm told, believe they can get closer to the essence of God through rituals and prayers that tap into spiritual energies. Some believe that such practices have the power to bring spiritual and emotional healing and, in some cases, to cure grave illnesses.

Rabbi Ephraim made a solemn entrance as he descended the stairs. A long, dark blue cape was draped over his shoulders. He had a beard. He was gracious and with a smile motioned for us to take a seat on the large couch.

"Tell me about Lee," he said, and he listened without taking his eyes from me as I spoke, nodding his head now and then.

When I finished telling him about Lee's illness and its progression, Ephraim said, "I would like to come and visit with Lee. After spending some time with him, I can determine if I will be able to help him."

I told him there wasn't much time. Lee was dying, and we had no idea how many days he had left.

"I will come to the hospital in two days," Ephraim said. And with that, he stood and showed us out. We left his house with a glimmer of hope. It was all we had.

Two days later, Ephraim came to the hospital. With his cape and brocaded cap, he stood out in the waiting room. Several people stared at Ephraim, then at us. We hurried him upstairs to Lee's room. Ephraim recited a prayer and then walked around Lee's bed several times with his eyes closed, mumbling words we couldn't decipher. I didn't know what to make of him. I'd never met anyone like Ephraim before. Was he truly a rabbi and a mystic? Was he a healer? Was he a crackpot? I had no idea. He seemed to want nothing in return for his assistance. I kept reminding myself that he had cured Howard.

Ephraim opened a brown leather satchel that looked like an old-fashioned doctor's bag. He took out a small burlap pouch and affixed it to the wall above Lee's head. We watched, perplexed and mesmerized, as he pulled out of the satchel a sprig of dried flowers. These he placed, along with a prayer written on a piece of paper, into the pouch on the wall over Lee's head.

Then Ephraim gave Wendy a small glass bottle filled with a brown liquid. "I want you to give Lee a half teaspoon of this in a glass of water, three times a day," he said. "I believe there is a chance Lee can be saved. I will go back to my congregation and select ten holy men, and every evening for the next eight days they will go to the ocean and pray. At the end of that time, we will wait for a sign as to whether Lee can be saved. I will call you when I have news."

I had my arm around Wendy's shoulder, and we nodded our agreement. Before leaving, Ephraim sat next to Lee for a few more minutes, reciting some prayers in Hebrew with his head bowed. Then he closed the worn leather satchel, shook our hands, and was gone.

It was an off-the-wall, outrageous notion that a faith healer could succeed where some of the best medical minds had been unable to help. The spectacle itself was no less bizarre. But it just might save Lee's life. Would Lee have been bothered by Ephraim? Would he have welcomed Ephraim's help? The last thing we wanted to do was add to our son's suffering. Lee hadn't been able to speak to us since his MRI in Boise. He couldn't ask, "What's going on?" Or, "Am I sick?" And we couldn't know which questions he might be asking himself, what he might be thinking. We didn't even know if he was aware of us. We didn't know if he could feel the touch of our hands.

We were making another decision for Lee because we didn't know what else to do.

Ten days later, we received a call from Ephraim. He wanted to come to the hospital and meet with us. When he arrived, we shook hands, and he walked over to Lee's bed. Placing one hand on Lee's head, and holding a bible in the other, he recited a prayer. This time, Lee's eyes were closed.

Then Ephraim turned to us. "After the holy men concluded their eight evenings of prayer, I received a sign from God that Lee's life can be saved," he said. "In order for this to happen, we must take the next steps."

"What does that mean?" I asked.

"First," said Ephraim, "the holy men who prayed at the ocean must be paid. Ten thousand dollars." He paused, perhaps expecting me to say something, but I was silent. "Next, we have to procure a Torah from the town of Safed in Israel and have it brought back here. Then, for a week I must pray every day at Lee's side reading from that Torah. And when I am finished, I believe you will find Lee getting better."

"How do I get a Safed Torah?" I asked. "And what will it cost?"

Ephraim told us that a Safed Torah would cost fifty thousand dollars. Plus, we'd need to pay for someone to fly to Israel to obtain the Torah and bring it back. The funds, he added, would need to be paid in advance. In cash.

Everything went cold inside me. In defiance of my skepticism, I had opened my heart to the possibility of a different kind of healing, something divine. But now it was mercenary, transactional, manipulative. I looked at Ephraim. His face was devoid of emotion and expression. I felt sick. I wanted to hurt him. I clenched my fists. Then I looked at Wendy.

"Wendy and I will need some time to think about this, and then we'll get back to you," I said. Lee was scheduled to leave NYU Medical Center the next morning to come home so he could spend his remaining days with his family, Criss, and his friends.

When Ephraim was gone, I turned to Wendy and said, "Wendy, this is crazy. It's a fraud." I had to fight to keep my voice calm. I did not want our conversation to spiral into something that could not be undone. This was a decision we needed to make together, and we both had to be fully on board with our choice, whatever it was.

I was convinced that Ephraim could not help Lee. His setup enraged me. There had been no talk of money until he assured us that Lee could be saved—as long as we paid up. I wondered how much Howard had been asked to pay Ephraim. I had assumed all along that we'd be expected to make a generous contribution of some kind. But to be taken advantage of in our most vulnerable moment, to have an extortionist put a price tag on a healing gift from God, was beyond anything I could have imagined.

But none of that mattered now. Wendy mattered. Her peace of mind. Our marriage.

"We're going to lose our son," Wendy said through tears. "And if there is *any* chance that what Ephraim wants to do can save Lee's life, we have to do it. I couldn't live knowing we had a chance to save Lee's life and didn't take it."

"We will do it," I said without hesitation. "We don't have to discuss it any further." I held her as she cried, and I put aside my doubts.

Two days after we brought Lee home to Connecticut, Ephraim arrived at our house with the Safed Torah and an overnight bag. He settled into Lee's room and placed a sleeping mat for himself at the foot of Lee's bed. He ate nuts and dried fruits and periodically emerged to eat fresh fruit from our kitchen and walk around the grounds of the house. Whenever we entered Lee's room, Ephraim would be sitting at Lee's side or on the floor reciting prayers, his head covered with a prayer shawl or yarmulke.

After three days, Ephraim informed us that he had to return to Brooklyn. This came as a surprise; he had been very clear about the need to pray at Lee's side for a week. The Jewish holiday Rosh Chodesh was approaching, he explained, so he had to return to his congregation. (Rosh Chodesh, I later learned, is a minor holiday that occurs at the beginning of every month.) He took the Torah with him and said he would continue to pray for Lee there.

I didn't hear from Ephraim again until two weeks after Lee passed away. His call came after Lee's funeral in New York, after we had accompanied our son's body on the flight to Idaho, after we had buried him in the small cemetery in Ketchum. It came while we were just beginning the process of trying to absorb that our son was gone forever.

"How is Lee doing?" he asked. "Have you noticed any progress in his recovery?"

It took me a few seconds to find my voice. "Lee died two weeks ago," I said. There was silence on the other end of the line.

"The Torah that we bought," I said. "I want it."

"I'm sorry. The Torah belongs here in the synagogue," Ephraim said.

Like hell it does. I told Ephraim that I would be in Brooklyn at 2 p.m. sharp the next day with my brother-in-law, Bob, to pick up the Torah, and if it wasn't there, I would return with the police.

When Bob and I arrived in Brooklyn, a woman opened the door and handed us the Torah. Ephraim was nowhere to be seen.

About a month after Lee's death, I considered reporting Ephraim to the fraud division of the New York Police Department. Who knows how many other vulnerable people he had defrauded? I didn't want more people to be taken advantage of. When I told Wendy what I was planning to do, she begged me to let it go.

"We've been through enough. The money's gone. It's done. I don't want to carry this on any longer," she said.

I had no doubt it was a scam—something I never would have believed I could fall for. But we were about to lose our child. I was willing to try anything. And would I do it again? Probably.

In the process of writing this book, I asked Margie if she could reach out to Howard, the man Ephraim had supposedly cured, to find out how he was doing. Was he still healthy, or had his HIV symptoms returned? Margie had lost touch with Howard over the years and was delighted to learn that he was doing well. I was happy to hear it, and surprised. Perhaps Ephraim's mystical healing wasn't a con. Or, maybe he was more complicated than that—a man with the ability to heal in ways we didn't understand, a man who was also greedy. I have no way of knowing.

Wendy and I donated the Torah to the Hillel House at Lafayette College, along with a donation for a reading room in Lee's memory.

Grief is consuming. Anger doesn't make it any easier. Wendy is a beautiful human being and a wise person, and she was right about leaving unnecessary burdens behind. Our son had died. We would focus our energies on keeping his memory alive in a positive way.

A LITTLE LESS than a year after Lee died, Wendy and I were sitting in the kitchen of our house in Connecticut on a Sunday evening eating Chinese takeout. We heard a crashing sound from the next room. We hurried into the den. Our eyes went to the couch table, on which a dozen or so framed family photos had been arranged. All but one had fallen over. The only frame still standing held a picture of Lee.

We looked at each other, speechless, and left the pictures untouched. A bit shaken, we returned to the kitchen and sat down again, not sure what to say to each other. But we didn't need to say anything. We didn't need to explain or make sense of it. We just let it be.

After clearing the dishes that night, we cracked open the two fortune cookies that had come with our meal. Both had the same message. *The stars come out at night. Everything is okay.*

I DECIDED TO scribble down the story of the seal a few years after Lee passed away. It took only half an hour for the story to pour out of me onto a yellow pad. The next day was Christmas, when our family would gather to exchange gifts. I had an idea. That evening, I sat down with our oldest grandchild, Eliza Lee, who was seven years old at the time. Together we looked at what I had written, and I asked her if she would like to read it to the family on Christmas morning.

The next morning, after we opened our gifts by the fireplace in the living room, I announced to the family that Eliza had something to read to us. She read carefully, her voice small and clear. When Eliza finished and looked up, the only sound in the room came from the crackling fire.

The reading of *The Sea and the Seal*, now a children's book illustrated by Heidi, has become a treasured ritual, a beautiful way to keep Lee with us. Every Christmas morning, after we open our gifts, we listen to the story of the seal, read by one of our grandchildren—Levi, Talia, Hope, Sam, or Eliza. Then Wendy and Heidi make stacks of pancakes, and we all crowd into the kitchen for breakfast. At Wendy's place at the table there is a small pile of gifts, every one having something to do with seals. We know that Lee is with us when we read the story and when Wendy opens her gifts. Time has a way of softening memories. But we do not forget.

Chapter 7

Beginning

Lee Pesky Learning Center officially opened its doors on February 3, 1997. We had two full-time employees, no clients, and very little understanding of what the future held in store.

It had been fourteen months and twenty-eight days since Lee passed away.

THE IDEA OF establishing a center in Lee's name dedicated to learning disabilities was born in the weeks before he died, in the house where he had grown up.

After we'd been told that nothing more could be done for Lee, we kept him at the hospital for a few more days. We were reluctant to let go of the possibility that the extraordinary people who had taken care of Lee—the doctors, nurses, orderlies, residents, and interns—might somehow still find a way to save him. By October 24, we knew it was time to take Lee home. We didn't know how much time he had left, but every day Lee could spend at home surrounded by his family in the house he had loved would be a blessing.

It was impossible for me to make sense of it all. The life we had been leading three months ago now seemed like another world. In that other world, my days had often started with an early morning trail run in the hills of Adam's Gulch, just beyond our house in Ketchum, followed by a cup of coffee at the Buckin' Bagel, Lee and Austin's bagel shop. I would watch Lee emerge from the kitchen, wiping his hands on his apron, to greet customers with a big smile and tell them about his latest bagel creation. Life was wonderfully mundane—routine business meetings, a quick drive to the market, a dinner party with friends. Or Wendy and I might have dinner at home, just the two of us, sitting on the deck with a glass of wine while watching a fly fisherman in the river below cast his line to the elusive trout that if caught would be returned to the river.

Above all, life for us was about family. I was always planning our next family adventure—a rafting trip down the Middle Fork of the Salmon River or a weeklong camping trip on horseback. Wendy was always planning our next family gathering—Thanksgiving dinner or the Christmas holidays. But it was a different world for us now.

We brought Lee home from the hospital to our house in Connecticut, where we had spent most of our time as a family. In preparation, the four of us had moved furniture, concert posters, books, picture frames, and the blue-and-white bedspread from Lee's room to the dining room. We wanted to recreate Lee's bedroom downstairs so he might be comforted by the look and feel of his favorite things around him, and where all of us—his family, Criss, and the hospice nurses—could care for him. The polished walnut dining table that we'd sat around for holiday dinners and special occasions of all kinds was gone. In its place, a hospital bed. And on a nearby side table, the ornate silver-framed photographs had been moved aside to make way for medications, including the Tegretol we had to have on hand in case Lee went into a seizure, which, we were warned, is a risk for patients with brain tumors. "You do not want to see that," the nurse said.

We had no idea to what extent Lee was aware of his surroundings or cognizant of us in his last few weeks. He needed full-time care and couldn't communicate with us. Could he hear us? We didn't know, but we still talked to Lee and took care never to converse with one another as if he weren't there.

We fed Lee, shaved him, and changed his pajamas. Every other day, Greg, Criss, and I gently lifted Lee out of bed and struggled to carry him up the stairs for a shower. One of us would hold Lee while he sat on a stool, and another one would wash him. These were tender, awkward, and oddly silly moments, as we invariably all got wet in the process.

In a cheap trick of nature, Lee looked fine, which made it even more difficult to accept the stark reality of the situation. Aside from the surgical hash marks on his bald head, there were no visible signs on his face or body that reflected the devastation inside him.

A week or so before Lee died, Wendy, Heidi, Greg, and I were having dinner in the kitchen as Lee slept in the adjoining dining room. For me, questions no one wanted to ask seemed to hover at the edge of our conversations: What do we do when Lee dies? What happens afterward?

These were unsettling questions. Even though we had acknowledged the medical certainty that Lee was dying, it was inconceivable to imagine him gone as long as he was still with us. That there would come a moment when Lee would simply no longer be there. Why should we—how could we—talk about Lee not being there when he was right here?

For two months, we had kept such thoughts to ourselves. But I knew that once Lee was gone, we would disperse and return to our lives. Diminished, certainly, but life would go on. We had always been a close family, and I wanted to find a way to keep Lee with us. For me, the time to talk about it was now.

Quietly, not wanting to upset Lee if he could indeed hear us, I said, "Let's think about doing something to keep Lee's memory alive. Create something that would be about Lee. Something we could feel good about."

We talked about the things Lee loved: Idaho, the outdoors, the mountains surrounding his home. Lee's joy in hiking, camping, skiing, and biking in the mountains had been apparent to all his family and friends. When the time would come for us to inscribe his tombstone in the small cemetery in Ketchum, we chose the words, *Among the mountains and stars Lee camps forever.* And below that, we added the three words that Wendy and I felt best described our son:

Smile Wit Love

As we talked about what we might do to honor Lee, our first thoughts turned toward the mountains: why not create a new hiking trail in Lee's name for people of all ages to enjoy and call it "Lee's Trail"? But the conversation continued, meandering along the path of Lee's life and everything he loved. The dirt bike he'd had as a teenager. Nice clothing (Lee was without a doubt the most stylish among us). Criss, the love of his life. Lee's chocolate lab, Tanner. A joke that crackled with dry wit. A powder day on the mountain.

Greg reminded us about Lee's favorite song, *Ripple*, by Jerry Garcia of the Grateful Dead. "That's right," we all nodded and couldn't help but smile. Although I disliked the Grateful Dead, I loved that song. Its chords had often drifted through the house from Lee's room. After Lee died, I would find myself humming the tune while on a hike or long run.

Our conversation trailed off.

"There is no one like Lee," Heidi said.

I thought about my middle child—the rebel and wit of our family. His sweet smile and his vulnerability. The things that were hard for Lee—achingly difficult—because of his learning differences and physical challenges. Heidi once remarked to me that when Lee was a kid, he went into most situations expecting to be the underdog, expecting to be misunderstood or discounted.

How many times when he struggled in school, I wondered, had Lee heard, "You didn't study enough," or "You're not paying enough attention"? I thought of the time Lee's headmaster told us Lee didn't belong at his school. The impact on Lee of his hidden disabilities could be brutal.

Lee's laborious handwriting, frequently illegible due to the unfortunate combination of dysgraphia and his small-motor issues, had not only made it difficult for him to keep up in class, but in one instance had earned him a veiled accusation of cheating. When Lee decided to retake the SATs after his first disappointing result, he was determined to do better, and he spent most of the summer studying to prepare himself with the help of a tutor. He was rewarded for his efforts with a much higher score the second time around.

But his significant improvement apparently set off an alarm bell for the testing service. "Lee's signature on this exam looks different than the one on his last exam," an official informed me on the phone. The implication: Lee must have had someone else take the test for him. "We're not accusing Lee of anything, but he'll have to take the exam again." We fought the decision and eventually vindicated Lee by providing proof of his dysgraphia. Lee and I never talked about it; around me, he kept his feelings to himself. But the episode must have been devastating for him.

One of the most painful memories I had of Lee's physical struggles was in senior year when his high school soccer coach left him on the bench for the final game of the season. Lee was the only kid on the team to sit out the whole game, which the team easily won. I was heartbroken for Lee and furious on his behalf. When I met the coach's eyes after the game, his look conveyed the unspoken message: "We had to win this game, and Lee might have jeopardized that." My first instinct was to tell the coach what I thought about his callousness. But I also realized that losing my cool and drawing further attention to the situation would have hurt my son even more than he probably already hurt. I held back and walked away with Lee. I wanted to hug him, but I didn't.

Not enough. Is that how the people around Lee made him feel when he was a kid? His teachers, his coaches, his family? Me? Is that what other kids with learning differences had to cope with? The feeling that whatever they did, no matter how hard they tried, wasn't enough? That *they* weren't enough?

I felt sick when I thought of how many times Lee must have felt left out, cut off, or let down when he was a kid simply because he didn't fit neatly within the outline of other people's expectations—including my own. I pushed my chair back from the table, went to the dining room-turned-bedroom, and sat down on the hospital bed next to Lee. I put my hand on his arm. My son's eyes were closed, his breath was steady, and his face was smooth—as if all his life's scars and cares had dropped away. But the tumor that had lain unseen and undetected in Lee for so long, mistaken for other ailments, hiding behind symptoms that should have meant something else, continued to grow quietly and spread its deadly tentacles.

Wendy, Greg, and Heidi looked up when I returned to the kitchen. "I have another idea," I said. "Let's do something to help kids with learning disabilities. An organization or foundation of some kind in Lee's name."

There was silence. Then both Heidi and Greg started talking, chiming in with questions and suggestions. Wendy watched as we batted the idea back and forth. She didn't say much, but I could see in her eyes, now filled with tears, that she loved the idea.

We agreed: We would honor Lee, in his name, in a way that would have had meaning for him and could benefit many others. We felt sure that Lee would have wanted and wholeheartedly approved of us helping children to lead their best lives. If there was anything in Lee's early life that prevented him from living to his fullest, it was his struggle with learning disabilities and being misunderstood by those of us around him.

I had no idea, as we sat talking in the kitchen that day, that I was taking the first step in what would be a fundamental shift for me. Until this point in my life, I had been driven largely by my desire to achieve, to provide for my family, and to take on yet another physical challenge. Recognition, too, was important for me. But now, I had a glimmer that there was more to life than more. The question of *how* I spent my time and how it might benefit others suddenly seemed far more urgent. Yes, I had always had a philanthropic bent. But this was not about where I was donating my money or how much. It was about where I was putting my heart.

In establishing a nonprofit to honor Lee, I was embarking on a mission that would absorb me for the remainder of my life. It was unexpected, surprising, and it would bring me a fulfillment deeper than virtually anything I had ever done.

WHEN MY FOUR partners and I decided to start our advertising agency, I was thirty-three years old. Wendy and I had two young children with the third on the way. In taking the leap to launch Scali, McCabe, Sloves, I was looking at the possibility of an empty bank account in nine months' time, which was roughly how long it would take us to run out of money if we couldn't convince clients to give us their business. But my partners and I were young, ambitious, hungry, and, among us, had enough experience to believe we could pull it off.

To be honest, I never really gave it a second thought at the time. I didn't like working for someone else, and I figured that owning a business would be the best way to achieve the level of financial security I wanted for my growing family. Subconsciously, I might have been inspired by my father—the man I had never aspired to be like when I was younger, the role model I had never wanted. But Lou Pesky had provided for his family, and he had worked hard in a tough trade to do it. I wanted the same thing, just in a different way. Though I wasn't a gambler like my father, I did take a big risk—and it paid off.

Starting Lee Pesky Learning Center posed far less of a financial risk than starting the agency, and thanks to the success of the agency and its sale fifteen years earlier, Wendy and I had resources to dedicate to an ambitious project. But I wasn't 33 anymore. I would be starting something new—a big something—at the age of 64. And I would soon find out that this venture was going to be vastly different and more complicated than anything I'd ever done.

I enjoy taking on challenges, especially when they are physical. I had run several marathons and spent a week traversing the Ruth Glacier in Alaska on skis. Wendy and I trekked and camped in Patagonia, and we traveled across Tibet in 1984 to join the American expedition at their base camp on Mount Everest. I was no stranger to trying new things. But this time, with the Lee Pesky Learning Center, I didn't have a clue what I was getting into.

Even when you're climbing a mountain like Kilimanjaro, which I did when I was fifty, you know exactly what you have to do, and you know (more or less) what you can expect. After all, many others have climbed it before you. Granted, you still have to haul yourself up the mountain, all 19,340 vertical feet of it, in five to eight days. But you can plan for it, train for it, pack for it, and psyche yourself up for it. If you've done your homework, you'll be familiar with the physical challenges you're likely to encounter: altitude sickness, blisters, exposure, dehydration, sore muscles, exhaustion, to name just a few. Climbing a big mountain, however—even the highest peak on the African continent—would, in hindsight, seem like a cakewalk compared with pouring my heart and soul into the non-profit learning center that would bear the name of our son.

If I hadn't been able to reach the summit of Kilimanjaro, if I'd had to turn back because of weather, an injury, or finding that I just wasn't strong enough, I would have been disappointed, but it would still have been an extraordinary experience. By the same token, if our fledgling advertising agency didn't get off the ground, I knew even then that I'd recover and move on, try again later, or get a job somewhere else. Not so with Lee Pesky Learning Center. Once I committed myself to it, there would be no turning back for me. Failure was not an option. This was about Lee. If I didn't succeed, it would be like losing Lee all over again and failing him once more.

Looking back, I can see that the deck was not stacked in our favor. My objective to establish a nonprofit learning center began with a wonderful idea: helping kids to overcome their learning disabilities. But unlike my mountain climbs or epic bicycle trips, I had only a vague plan to start with and no road map. As parents, Wendy and I dealt firsthand with the challenges of learning disabilities, but we weren't education professionals, nor were we versed in the field of neuroscience. And while we had the money to get something going, I had no idea how much I'd have to invest over the long term to make it a sustainable nonprofit. What's more, we wanted to establish the learning center in Idaho, a state with a poor track record in prioritizing education.

There were so many reasons *not* to do it. We could have simply made a meaningful donation in Lee's name to the National Center for Learning Disabilities, an outstanding organization on whose board I would serve several years later. But I wanted to have a direct, hands-on impact in helping kids like Lee and their families. We had witnessed Lee's confusion and frustration and had experienced the anguish of not being able to help him. By the time Lee died, research and science about learning disabilities had made substantial strides, but far too many children were still falling through the cracks of the education system. The need was glaring, galling, and urgent.

You have to ask yourself: why does a nation that developed one of the world's greatest public education systems have so many children who still don't learn—or aren't taught—to read, write, or do math with the proficiency they need to thrive? I thought of Charles Dickens's words in *A Tale of Two Cities*: "It was the best of times, it was the worst of times." That's where we were—and still are—with education in our country. We have a firm handle on the science of learning, and we know what works in addressing literacy challenges. We are a rich country. Yet millions of kids aren't benefiting from the abundance. The science makes its way slowly and unevenly to the classrooms. And, in my view, the main culprits for inequitable access to education are racism and poverty. This disparity is an uncomfortable and universal truth that stares each of us in the face every day in so many critical areas: hunger, health care, education—to name just a few.

For me, the sense of failure was not just global, but personal. I felt it deep within, in a place hollowed out by the loss of Lee, where grief and uncomfortable thoughts bumped up against each other. Had I done enough for Lee? Even after we learned about his learning and motor challenges, just how understanding was I? I was grieving, still trying to fathom the loss of our child. Somehow, though, I knew that my grieving Lee would be closely bound with establishing and nurturing a center in his name.

It's been twenty-five years since Lee died, and grief still surprises me. It's not something you get better at. What I *have* learned so far is that how one mourns and copes with loss seems to be different for each one of us. Over the years, I've sat with many other parents who have lost children, and the only things we all seem to have in common are the loss and the certainty that it will stay with us for the rest of our lives. I don't believe that losing a child is something that you ever get over. Rather, the hole you feel inside you shifts its shape over time. Somehow, you learn to live with it, each of us finding resilience in our own way.

Wendy and I chose not to live in the past, but not to forget it, either. We keep Lee within the circle of our family. We continue to talk about him, not in hushed voices, but openly, fondly, sometimes even boisterously. When people ask us how many children we have, Wendy and I always say, "Three. We have three children." Over time, the pain for us has become less intense, less consuming, but it has never gone away. And it never will.

In the beginning, we took one breath, one step, one hour, one day at a time. Wendy dealt with it quietly, with the poise and calm she brings to nearly everything she does. But she also had her moments. A couple of months after Lee died, we were attending a wedding rehearsal dinner for the son of our close friends, the Marvins. Steven was about the same age as Lee, and they had been friends. In the middle of dinner, Wendy turned to me and said, "Let's get out of here." She did not need to tell me why. We politely excused ourselves and left.

Or there would be times when we were driving and a song came on the radio, and tears would roll down her cheeks. Wendy is the strongest and most tender person I know.

My immediate response to the death of our son was to act. To move. To fix something. To make amends. Helping kids in a way I couldn't—in the way I didn't—help Lee. In that sense, I was fortunate: for me, the loss of Lee became a doorway to understanding and helping people like Lee, which, in turn, helped me to better understand my son, my relationship with him, and, ultimately, myself.

Chapter 8

Serendipity

"The coincidences surrounding this whole project are almost eerie. It feels like we have all come together in this spot to fulfill some higher purpose . . . to make a difference . . . to touch lives in some meaningful and loving way."

—Blossom Turk, Lee Pesky Learning
Center Journal, June 6, 1996

Within six weeks of Lee's death, I had fully immersed myself in the process of absorbing everything I could about learning disabilities and the science of education and reading.

Wendy, Heidi, and Greg were fully committed to the idea, but they had far less time available than I did to devote to such a consuming project. Heidi had just had her first child, Wendy was coowner of a thriving business and was shuttling back and forth to be with Heidi and the baby, and Greg was in his first year of business school. Had I asked for help, I know they would have given it. But my family probably understood how much I needed to throw myself into creating something in Lee's name.

Once Lee Pesky Learning Center was up and running, they would each play an important role in its development. Wendy took full charge of our annual fundraising event for several years. Greg served on the Board for eighteen years and recently took the helm as Chairman. Heidi, too, has always been ready to jump in, applying her considerable talents to help with marketing and design. Most important, over the years the contributions of dedicated staff members, energetic board members, and thousands of donors have come together to bring Lee Pesky Learning Center to where it is today.

But at the beginning, I was on my own, and it became my full-time occupation.

My first stop was the Stern Center for Language and Learning in Burlington, VT, established in 1983 by Dr. Blanche Podhajski. We knew about the Stern Center through Wendy's parents, who had been leading supporters of Blanche's work because of their strong ties to the Burlington community and their dedication to education. In 1996, there were only a handful of independent facilities in the country that could diagnose learning disabilities, provide individual remediation services, and offer resources and training for teachers and others involved in education—all under one roof. The Stern Center was one of the few.

"Tell me everything you can about learning disabilities and what you do here," I asked Blanche when we sat down. She then shared everything she could about the diagnostic, intervention, and teaching models used by the Stern Center. Blanche also shared her insights about some of the pitfalls I might encounter. In creating an independent learning center that would intersect with the public school system and impact its students, we might be viewed with skepticism. School districts, she warned, could be reluctant to engage with a private nonprofit and a newcomer to the field.

This didn't surprise me. As a trustee of both my alma maters and a couple of private secondary institutions, I had observed that educators can be protective of their turf. I can understand that teachers and education professionals might respond to changes (even positive ones) with suspicion or defensiveness. Most of them are in the unenviable position of having to meet the growing expectations and demands of parents, school boards, and legislators, within an environment of incessant budget cuts and ever-shrinking resources. All while trying to do their best for their students. Teachers can be among the most valuable and least appreciated players in the lives of our children. That's the reason Wendy and I chose to create The Pesky Award for Inspirational Teaching at Boise State

University. Every graduating student in the College of Education can nominate a K–12 teacher who inspired them to seek a career in teaching, and four teachers are chosen for the award every year and are honored at graduation. Wouldn't it be terrific if more colleges of education did something similar?

Blanche also emphasized the importance of building strong partnerships with state agencies. The Stern Center had worked tirelessly to strengthen relationships not only with public schools, but also with agencies of education and the Vermont legislature.

"Anything else?" I asked.

"Yes," she responded. "You'll need a very good executive director. Make sure you find the right one."

The orientation I got from Blanche and others at the Stern Center that day gave me a good start. It also reminded me how much I didn't know. And for now, I had no partners to lean on or to brainstorm with, as I'd had at Scali, McCabe, Sloves. It was daunting, nutty, and fun in a scary kind of way. Matthew Weatherley-White, one of our first board members, has remarked that I approached the launching of Lee Pesky Learning Center (LPLC) with "an open spirit of inquiry." That's a very charitable way to put it.

Even after the first few years, by which time we had recruited many outstanding specialists and professionals to join our staff, we were still finding our way, learning and course-correcting as we progressed. "Building the plane while we were flying it" might be the most accurate way to put it. That's how Dr. Anne Clohessy describes it now. Anne is a psychologist and has been LPLC's Lead Evaluator for fifteen years.

I WOULDN'T ENCOURAGE anyone to establish and build a nonprofit the way we did—by the seat of our pants. But serendipity would grace Lee's project just enough to keep it going and growing. And the first great serendipitous stroke came to us in the form of a woman with the grand name of Blossom Turk.

Early on, I decided that our learning facility should be located in Boise rather than in the Wood River Valley, where Lee had lived. Our beautiful and remote valley includes four towns that in 1996 had a combined population of less than 17,000 (today, we're up to a whopping 23,000). Since we hoped to reach as many children as possible across the state and to be able to draw on the resources of a city, the center needed to be based in Boise, the state capital and the largest city in Idaho.

I'd been searching for months for an executive director who could help me shape the plan and run Lee Pesky Learning Center, but I hadn't yet found the right person. I was getting impatient. I wanted to get the damn thing going, and there was no way I could do it by myself. What it came down to in the end was a bit of luck and a lot of gut instinct.

"You know," an acquaintance in Boise said when I griped to her about still not having found a director, "it might be a long shot, but you should talk to Blossom Turk. She has thirty years under her belt in Idaho public schools and recently retired as the principal of Boise High School."

"Does she know anything about learning disabilities?" I asked.

"No idea," she shrugged. "But if you're looking for someone who's highly respected in education here in Idaho, you couldn't do better. Everyone knows and trusts her." Blossom, she added, was apt to show up at high school basketball games wearing sweatpants, and she was always one of the loudest to cheer.

That sounded promising. I wanted someone who, like me, would be passionate and excited about what we would be doing. And, as a bonus, this woman loved basketball.

The legendary Blossom agreed to meet with me for lunch, even though she was in the process of packing up her life in Boise, selling her house, and moving to Portland to be near her son and grandchildren. She met with me, she later confided, on a lark.

The woman who walked into the restaurant and introduced herself had a warm, easy smile, and an elegance that comes from being utterly at ease with oneself.

"Please don't take this the wrong way," I said, my smart mouth taking over before my better sense kicked in, "but when I first saw your name, Blossom Turk, I wondered if you were also a female wrestler."

Now you've done it, Alan, I groaned to myself. *What a dumb remark.*

But Blossom laughed and, in an accent that could only come from New York City, admitted that there might be similarities between teaching and wrestling. We hit it off immediately.

Blossom was an experienced educator, bright, personable, and tough. What she didn't know about learning disabilities, I figured she could learn. Most important, as a highly respected "insider" of the public school system, she could help us build trust with teachers, school administrators, and parents—partners who would be critical to the future success of Lee Pesky Learning Center.

She and I were about the same age, came from the Bronx, and had attended public schools in New York. Had we known each other in high school, I'm sure Blossom and I would have been friends. By the end of the lunch, we were practically finishing each other's sentences.

After our meeting, Blossom called her son to let him know she had changed her mind. She wasn't moving to Portland.

"I've decided to stay in Boise to start a learning center," she told him. "I'm going to take a chance and fly with this guy, Alan Pesky."

In the years that followed, Blossom loved telling her colleagues at LPLC the story of how we first met. "When I walked out of that lunch, I felt like someone had shot electricity through my body. This guy was so passionate about the idea and the mission, I knew I had to work with him in starting the Center."

I'm guessing she also told everyone that I'd asked if she was moonlighting as a wrestler.

I HIRED BLOSSOM in May, before I even knew what we were creating, what it would look like, or what exactly it would offer. I asked her to start by learning as much as she could about learning disabilities. Then she would work with me to put together a business plan and to get ready to open our doors the following winter. We agreed not to lock ourselves into a specific configuration until we felt we had enough solid information to craft a good plan. We had a lot to learn.

My thoughts about what our nonprofit should offer were influenced by the experience Wendy and I had had with Lee. I tried to put myself in the shoes of parents who would be coming to us for help. What would they be looking for and what kind of information would they need to understand the challenges their child was experiencing? How would they like their child to feel when entering Lee Pesky Learning Center for the first time? How could they best support their child in the process? Blossom and I agreed the essentials would consist of evidence-based diagnoses and clinical services, counseling for the kids and their families, and accurate and up-to-date information about learning disabilities that could be shared with educators.

These were ambitious goals that we'd need to map out and clearly define. The physical space for Lee Pesky Learning Center would also be important, as we wanted to create a welcoming environment for children and their families. And it had to be located in an area that was easily accessible to parents who would be driving their children to LPLC before or after school.

Then there were the details one is likely to gloss over while brainstorming the grand plan. We had to incorporate and register as a nonprofit, find an accountant, get phone lines and utilities sorted out, buy office equipment, order stationery. The tedious, nitty-gritty stuff still needs to be done even when you want to change the world.

We also needed a name. Wendy and I first agreed it should be The Lee David Pesky Center for Learning Enrichment. It was, admittedly, a mouthful. Even though we never really used our kids' middle names, I was unwilling at that point to give up anything related to Lee—even his middle name. I felt strongly that the name had to be all about Lee and should describe what we would be offering. A few years later, it was suggested to us that the Center would benefit from a shorter, more user- and design-friendly name: Lee Pesky Learning Center. By then, what we'd built already embodied Lee's spirit so fully that having Lee's middle name associated with it no longer felt important to me.

I always made a point of referring to it as Lee Pesky Learning Center rather than the "Pesky Center," and I still do. I correct people if they use the abbreviated version, as I don't want them to think LPLC is about me or our family name. It should always be about Lee and kids like him.

Between the two of us, Blossom and I covered an enormous amount of ground in those first few months. Blossom attended scientific and academic conferences, consulted with specialists in the field, and spent hundreds of hours speaking with teachers in Boise's public schools and meeting with parents of kids with learning disabilities. I reached out to state legislators, people at the State Department of Education, and business leaders I had met during my twenty years in Idaho.

Ironically, my one business failure would prove invaluable to me in laying some of the groundwork for Lee Pesky Learning Center and in raising money. Shortly after I retired and Wendy and I made the decision to spend most of our time in Idaho, I started a magazine publishing company in Ketchum called Peak Media, whose flagship publication would be the state magazine, *Oh, Idaho*. Unfortunately, I had to pull the plug on it after seven years, having underestimated the investment needed to make it economically viable. Nonetheless, I loved my work for the magazine. Dressed in comfortable shoes, khakis, V-neck sweater, and bowtie, I drove all over Idaho to get the word out about the publication and drum up advertisers. I met small business owners, heads of major corporations, presidents of Idaho's universities, state representatives, and Idaho's US Congress members and senators. I even got to know Governor Cecil Andrus, whom we persuaded to write the introduction for each issue of the magazine. On my road trips to places like Pocatello, Blackfoot, and Coeur d'Alene, I'd stay at motels and eat at friendly small-town diners.

It was a monumental but welcome change from the tightly buttoned-up, glamorous world of New York City, Paris, London, and Tokyo—just some of the many cities I was regularly traveling to as president of Scali, McCabe, Sloves International. I loved getting to know the sprawling state of Idaho—how the different communities related to one another, how the state government operated, and who the business leaders were.

Financially, Peak Media was a flop. The experience, on the other hand, couldn't have been more valuable, paying back in spades when I was setting up Lee Pesky Learning Center. By the time I was approaching people throughout the state to garner support for LPLC, I wasn't an outsider. I knew exactly whom to call in the legislature about my plans for LPLC, and I had an inside track on potential donors, corporate sponsors, and possible board members. What I had thought of as a failure turned out to be the best preparation I could have had for establishing a nonprofit organization in Idaho.

The response Blossom and I received about our plan for a learning center was overwhelmingly positive for the simple reason that there was nothing in Idaho that even came close to what we envisioned. Idaho was noticeably deficient in its support of students with learning differences, and its overall spending per student in the area of public education consistently ranked at or near the bottom of the country.

The capacity for addressing learning challenges in schools differed widely from state to state, but I was surprised to discover that most of the neighboring states didn't have all-in-one facilities dedicated to helping kids with learning disabilities, either. This included Montana, Wyoming, Nevada, Utah, and Oregon. Parents who were seeking help for their kids with learning challenges could, with luck, find the necessary services, but they would be piecemeal and dispersed. For example, you could have your child diagnosed by some psychologists or at certain clinics, find counseling from a handful of qualified therapists, and locate special education professionals who could provide one-on-one remediation sessions for your child. But nowhere in those six states (including Idaho) could you find these essential services together in one facility.

When Blossom and I were laying the groundwork for LPLC, about 30 percent of Idaho residents over the age of sixteen were reported to be deficient in language and math skills, and the state's high school dropout rate hovered around 33 percent. These gaps were not due solely to unaddressed learning disabilities, but the statistics certainly underscored the need for the services our facility would provide to schoolchildren in our state. And the value of having a nonprofit institution that would bring together a team of professionals under one roof handling all aspects of learning disabilities is hard to overstate. The holistic approach that Blossom sketched out for us would be groundbreaking not only in Idaho, but for the entire region, as well.

It became clear in those first few months that Blossom and I would have to keep stirring pots on many different burners all at the same time to get LPLC going by the following winter. Among the priorities we were juggling, nothing was more important than the quality of the care LPLC would provide. To reach as many kids as possible, we had to establish credibility, which in turn meant that everything we did had to be exemplary. And exemplary for us meant that our methodology and services must be grounded in science and bring demonstrable benefits to the kids.

We were going to be dealing with children who, like Lee, were vulnerable. And with families who were fragile from the worry and stress that came with trying to understand why their child was having difficulties learning. We would be working with people who were desperate for answers and who would be putting their faith in us. It was imperative that everything we did would affirm their confidence in LPLC.

I KNEW THAT we'd have to get rock-solid advice from people who were at the forefront of research and clinical expertise on learning disabilities. That's when I thought of Dr. Sally Shaywitz. Wendy and I had met Sally thirteen years earlier. She had helped Lee when the Educational Testing Service challenged his SAT results based on the illegibility of his signature. Sally had examined and tested Lee, then prepared a comprehensive report on his learning disabilities, which included dysgraphia. With her testimony, and the help of a handwriting expert and a good attorney, we were able to convince the SAT officials that Lee's scores should be accepted.

I had no idea if Sally would remember me or how I would even get in contact with her again. Through a trail of phone calls, I finally located her office at Yale Medical School and left a vague message with her assistant, asking if Sally could please call me back. When I got her on the phone a few days later, her voice was friendly and upbeat. "I'm so happy to hear from you, Alan! How's Lee doing? He's such a lovely young man. I hope everything is going well for him."

It had only been about six months since Lee had died. Conversations like these were not unusual. But the first few words always caught in my throat. I told Sally that Lee had passed away. The reason I was calling,

I explained, was that Wendy and I would be starting a learning center named for Lee in Boise, Idaho.

"I've hired a wonderful woman who'll be running it," I said, before my voice could crack again. "Her name is Blossom Turk, and she's from New York. I think you'd like her. She's had a long, illustrious career in education, but she's not a special ed teacher. So, we need help." I asked Sally if it would it be possible for Blossom, Wendy, and me to visit with her and learn about her work at Yale and anything she could share with us about the latest developments in the field of learning disabilities.

Sally, along with her husband, Bennett, had for many years been one of the leading specialists in the field of learning disabilities, particularly dyslexia. She and Bennett are cofounders and codirectors of the Yale Center for Dyslexia & Creativity. In 1983, Sally launched the groundbreaking and still ongoing *Connecticut Longitudinal Study*, which tracks a large random sample of students from kindergarten into adulthood—including typical readers and those with dyslexia.[10] Over the years, the study has provided valuable data about the prevalence and persistence of dyslexia.[11] Also interesting to me was that they were tracking the long-term impact of dyslexia on adults, including economic and other life consequences.

Sally agreed to meet with us and mentioned a date the following month when she would have a couple of hours available in her schedule. It was a long way for us to travel for a two-hour meeting, but I knew how busy Sally was and was grateful for any time she could spare.

A few hours later, our phone rang again.

"Alan, it's Sally." I don't recall her exact words, but the gist was "Coming all the way from Idaho for such a short meeting is crazy. What you and Wendy are talking about doing is important. I've spoken with Bennett, and we're both clearing our schedules for the entire day for you."

When we arrived a few weeks later for the visit, she and Bennett took us through as much as they could, in what amounted to a crash course on dyslexia. Sally also happened to have a brain scan scheduled at the end of that day for a child with a learning disability. That was an eye-opener for me.

Researchers had recently begun using *f*MRI scans to see which areas of the brain are active during reading, writing, math, and other learning tasks, and which parts of the brain *are not* firing for people with learning or attention issues. "These scans," Sally said, "have shown that the part of the brain dealing with reading works differently in people who have dyslexia, that there is a neural signature for dyslexia—an inefficient functioning of the systems in the back of the left side of the brain which facilitates fluent, automatic reading."

Here's a simplified way to think about how information processing in the brain works, and how we explain it now at LPLC when we meet with parents: Imagine a pipeline to illustrate the flow of information through the mind of a learner. Information flows through the brain like water through a pipe. When the ends of the pipe are as wide as the middle, information can flow smoothly into the learner's mind to be used for reasoning or storing in memory, and then flow back out, unimpeded, in the form of a written or oral response. For people who have disabilities that affect the *input* end, the opening of the pipeline is bottlenecked, and despite strong reasoning and/or memory skills in the middle of the pipe, processing is slowed at the beginning, leaving the learner stymied in taking in information or working through complex instructions at a typical rate. For people who have disabilities that affect the *output* end, a bottleneck may result in trouble coming up with an answer, reading fluently, or completing written work under time pressure. Lee experienced challenges on both the input end (due to auditory processing issues) and on the output end with writing (due to dysgraphia).

Unfortunately, this is invisible to people around kids with learning differences. It had been invisible to me. As Sally was showing us around, I found myself thinking of Lee and all the times I had pushed him to try harder. Even after he had been diagnosed, however imperfectly, I still had a hard time believing that Lee couldn't just "power through it."

Sally explained that once a kid like Lee has been evaluated and diagnosed, you realize that he has probably been trying his best yet is still not able to get the results he was aiming for, to say nothing of the effect of having an anxious adult looking over his shoulder. A few years after we opened LPLC, I came across an article about Sally in the publication *Educational Leadership*. Just as she had explained to us when we visited her at Yale, she described in the interview how MRI technology has improved our understanding of reading and dyslexia. "Now, we can look at an imaging pattern and say, 'Aha, this is a real problem; this is as real as a broken arm that you might look at on an X-ray.'"[12]

But the reality is far more complex than fixing a broken bone. How various processing elements of the brain interact with one another and contribute to learning can vary greatly from person to person. This is just as true for people who don't have learning disabilities. Some people, for example, use visual-spatial thinking to do math problems, while others rely more on language, counting to find the answer. (Some of my friends, whom I will not name, use their fingers.)

In the same interview, Sally pointed out that language is instinctive for humans in a way that reading is not. "We know that whereas speaking is natural, reading is not. Children do not automatically learn to read," she said. "Put a baby in a speaking environment and that child will learn to speak. We don't have to teach children how to talk."[13] (The exception is the small percentage of people who suffer from a significant language disorder.) Writing—and therefore, by extension, reading—is a relatively "recent" development in human history, going back only about 5,000 years. There still exist a surprising number of societies in the world that have no or scant written language.

The point is that the human brain is not hardwired to read—something I never knew. Yet, despite this fact, we teach reading in schools as if learning to read were as natural as learning to speak. I was coming to understand in our session with Sally and Bennett that all of our brains, whether we struggle with learning differences or not, are imperfectly equipped to learn to read and write. Everyone has a unique learning fingerprint, and people like Lee with learning disabilities are simply at the outer edges of the bell curve of human brain function.

At the end of our day with Sally and Bennett, our heads were spinning. We had been lucky enough to spend time with two of the most prominent experts in the field of special education, and we were encouraged by what we had learned: advanced diagnostic testing approaches were now available, and evidence-based practices with proven results could be used to create intervention plans adapted to the specific needs of individual kids with learning disabilities.

The bottom line: If we set our center up correctly, we could make a huge difference in the lives of kids who struggled with learning differences. What's more, we would be doing it in a largely rural and underserved state. We would be able to help kids like Lee in a way that Wendy and I hadn't been able to help him. Blossom, Wendy, and I felt optimistic about what lay ahead.

THINGS WERE COMING together in an almost miraculous way, as Blossom noted in the journal she kept about our first several months. "At the risk of sounding like a devotee of the 'Age of Aquarius,' this whole project and its progression seem guided by some invisible, loving, and powerful force that is helping to create it," she wrote.

We were getting enthusiastic support from specialists and researchers in the field, finding sympathetic ears in the Idaho legislature, recruiting great board members, and, thanks to Blossom, winning over public-school officials. So I was taken aback by some of the reactions we got from potential corporate donors.

I had managed to line up a lunch meeting with the CEO of a multinational corporation that was one of the largest employers in Boise. The young man listened politely as we explained our plans for LPLC. "We're going to work with kids who have learning differences, and we're going to help these kids fulfill their potential in life by becoming successful, lifelong learners," Blossom said, concluding our pitch on an upbeat note.

"You know, I'll be very honest with you," the CEO said. "I'm not interested in kids who have learning problems. I'm interested in kids who are bright and who are going to go on to benefit the type of work that we do here—the engineers, the scientists, and so on. That's what I'm interested in."

It was a short meeting.

As we walked out of the restaurant, Blossom turned to me and said, "What an asshole."

I laughed, liking her all the more for her honesty. "Never mind," I said. "I've got plenty more prospects on my list."

That meeting was an important reminder that misconceptions about learning disabilities were still widespread—even among business leaders, who, one would think, ought to know better. This would have to be a part of LPLC's mission, too: making accurate information available to the general public. We planned to organize conferences, write op-ed pieces, do interviews with journalists, and make presentations at schools and to parent groups. To support our work with individual children, LPLC staff and Board would continually need to get the word out about what learning differences are and how they can manifest and affect people.

Why should we, as a society, care about children with learning issues? First, we're talking about a large number of people. As I've mentioned, research indicates that 15–20 percent of the population experience symptoms of learning disabilities. In other words, between 50 and 65 million people struggle with learning in some fashion.

Second, as any teacher can tell you, reading is the fundamental skill on which all formal education depends: kids begin by learning to read, and then they read to learn. This means that when a child falls behind in reading, the gap is not static but continues to widen. As other children forge ahead, a student with unidentified learning disabilities has not yet mastered the essential skills needed to thrive in school.

The personal toll can be devastating. Dr. Julianne Masser is a former client of LPLC and is now a child psychologist specializing in learning issues. She shared what it was like for her as a child struggling with dyslexia: "I felt stupid, bad at school, and stigmatized. Even as a six-year-old, I knew I was falling behind other kids, stuttering over the ten words I was asked to read out loud. I often felt isolated and dumb."

Yet Julianne considers herself fortunate. "Unlike most kids who face dyslexia, I was born to two medical doctors who had the means to support the intervention that would make me a successful student. I was also lucky because I was a six-year-old struggling to learn in Boise, Idaho—an extremely unlikely place for a center that helps kids like me." LPLC, Julianne believes, gave her a safe place to develop lifelong learning skills, determination, and resiliency. "Lee Pesky Learning Center saved my life," she said.

If you happen to be a child with learning differences but—unlike Julianne or Lee—don't have a family with the resources to get you the help you need to overcome the challenges or to give you a leg up, you might very well be looking at a different kind of life. Students with learning disabilities are more than twice as likely to be suspended as their classmates without disabilities, and they drop out of high school at nearly three times the rate of all students.[14] They are also more likely to turn to drugs and alcohol.

And that's just high school. In adulthood, the consequences of significant learning disabilities that go unaddressed can become even more severe. Adults with learning disabilities are twice as likely to be jobless than those who don't.[15] There's also an alarming correlation between learning disabilities and incarceration: about half of the prison population in the US has some form of learning disability.[16]

The social and economic costs to society of inadequately addressed literacy challenges (including learning disabilities) are enormous. They include remediation programs in public schools that often come too late to be effective and the remedial reading, writing, and math skills training American businesses have to provide for their employees. Three years after we opened LPLC, the Mackinac Center for Public Policy in Michigan estimated that the cost to our economy of the lack of basic skills among students is around $16 billion a year.[17] Gaps in learning also impact our national security: nearly 70 percent of Americans between the ages of 17 and 24 are deemed ineligible for military service—a quarter of those because of literacy and aptitude issues, the rest because of health challenges or criminal records.[18]

When you look at it in these macroterms, the scale of our nation's literacy challenges seems insurmountable. How could a small learning center, kick-started in the largely rural state of Idaho by a retired couple without a background in education, neuroscience, or child psychology, hope to make a difference?

We didn't know. But we had to start somewhere.

LEE PESKY LEARNING Center opened for its first day of business in a modest, bright office space. A large, framed picture of Lee at the age of eight, with his big toothy grin, hung to the right of the reception desk. We had two staff members: Blossom and Deb Glaser, who was one of the most highly qualified professionals in special education at the time in Boise. At the beginning, we were limited to conducting evaluations, providing diagnoses, and offering one-on-one remediation sessions.

Three days after we opened Lee Pesky Learning Center, Blossom called me, concerned.

"No one has called us yet," she said. No parents, no teachers. Maybe we have to do more to make people aware of who we are and the services we provide."

"They'll come," I assured her. "Just be patient."

"Shouldn't we run some advertising?" she persisted.

My knowledge at that time about learning disabilities was still somewhat limited. I was, however, an expert in advertising, having spent twenty years in the advertising business. I probably knew as much as anyone about marketing and how to convince people to buy a product. But I didn't think advertising was the right way for us to bring in clients.

We weren't selling Volvo cars or Perdue chickens. Lee Pesky Learning Center was in the business of improving lives and, in some cases, even saving lives. The best way for us to tell our story would be through parents who had seen the benefits of effective remediation in their children and then told others about the work we were doing. One by one, case by case, success by success. Our advertising would be word of mouth.

I had confidence in our small team and the quality of the help they could offer kids and their families. I was convinced that if we proved to be good at what we were doing, word would get out. A terrific article had been written about us by the *Idaho Statesman* and appeared in the paper the day we opened. That would surely help, I thought. The reporter had done a great job capturing what we were all about.

A week later, Blossom called again.

"Alan," she said. "We still don't have clients."

Chapter 9

The Place Where It Arose

Day One at Scali, McCabe, Sloves, May 1, 1967: We had no clients. My partners—Marvin, Ed, Sam, Len—and I sat at our desks in the first corporate offices of our new agency: two rooms on the 9th floor of the Gotham Hotel on 55th Street and Fifth Avenue. We made a lot of phone calls, waited for potential clients to call back, and rearranged items on our desks. The phone rang only once that day. It was reception calling to let us know there was someone downstairs to see us. Could they send the visitor up? We jumped up when the door opened, eager to greet our first prospect. It was Len's wife. She had come to drop off a chocolate cake. At least we had cake.

Over the next few days, calls trickled in from friends, acquaintances, and the curious. A reporter at *Advertising Age,* the most high-profile industry publication at the time, called.

"So, Ed, what's going on?" the reporter asked Ed McCabe.

"Nothing," Ed said, lounging in his chair. He may have had his feet on the desk. Ed was our copywriter and, of the five partners, the most well known.

"Aren't you getting nervous?" the reporter pressed.

"Not at all," Ed replied. "Sooner or later someone with brains will give us their account. Scali, McCabe, Sloves is going to be around for a *long* time."

Marvin and I exchanged looks. Ed was a brilliant copywriter, and he was cocky. But Marvin and I weren't worried, either. The five of us had solid experience in advertising and a good balance of strengths and talents. Two weeks before we opened, the prestigious Gold Key Awards ceremony had taken place at the Waldorf Astoria. Ed, who at that time worked with the Carl Ally agency, walked off with three top awards for copywriting. An *Advertising Age* headline proclaimed, "Gold Key Ceremony Echoes with News of the McCabe Shop."[19] By "McCabe shop," they meant our new agency, Scali, McCabe, Sloves. The timing could not have been better.

THE IDEA FOR Scali, McCabe, Sloves (SMS) grew out of a chance conversation six months earlier. Marvin, Len, and I found ourselves together in the elevator one evening. We worked at the Papert, Koenig, Lois advertising agency, or PKL as it was known in the trade. It had been a tough day for Marvin Sloves and Len Hultgren. The griping started before the elevator door closed, and it continued as we walked north on Third Avenue.

Marvin was furious about a phone call he'd had with George Lois, the art director on the Xerox account and one of the founding partners of PKL. Marvin, the account supervisor, had flown to Rochester that morning to present the new campaign to Xerox. Their VP of advertising liked the ads but insisted on a few changes to the visual in the lead ad. General feedback from clients was expected; micromanagement of the artwork by clients was unusual. But Xerox was not the usual corporate account. Xerox revolutionized the photo-copier market with the introduction of the first desktop plain-paper copier in 1963. Within a few years, they had captured 97 percent of the rapidly growing world market.[20] In the advertising world, Xerox was one of the most coveted accounts in the country.

"Marvin, why not call George now," the Xerox VP said, gesturing to the phone on the conference table. "I think you should tell him right away about the changes I want him to make."

"Sure," Marvin replied, bracing himself as he dialed the number. George Lois was the director of PKL's creative department, and creative directors of top agencies could be very touchy when their work was challenged. George wasn't touchy. He was volcanic.

With the phone to his ear, Marvin nodded and smiled as George tore into him. He hoped the Xerox executive couldn't hear George's tirade.

"George shouted at me that it was a great ad, that he wouldn't change it," Marvin told us. "He said if the VP didn't like it, well, then tough luck. Can you imagine the dance I had to do to leave that office without losing our biggest account?"

Len rarely got worked up about anything, but that night he piped in with his own complaints. He'd come to loggerheads with the creative department about one of his research studies. Len lived by numbers, statistics, and focus group findings. He gave us a brief lecture about the perils of shoddy or—even worse—sham research. "These guys want our research to justify a decision they've already made. I don't work that way," he said.

My day, to be honest, had been pretty good. I just listened as they vented.

"That place is a madhouse," Marvin declared. "We have some of the biggest and most important clients in the country, and they run their shop like a delicatessen."

He wasn't wrong. PKL was a powerhouse of creativity, but the management was, in our view, erratic. Creative genius doesn't necessarily translate to savvy business management. Still, we would be surprised a few years after we left when PKL shuttered its doors. In a matter of nine years, they had dazzled the industry and became the first agency to go public. And then they were gone. A cautionary tale of the fragility of celebrity in advertising.

We reached the corner of 66th, and I needed to catch the crosstown bus to West End Avenue, where Wendy and I lived. I looked at my watch, hoping I hadn't missed the bus. "If you guys feel so strongly about it," I said, "why don't you just start your own agency?"

Marvin stared at me for a moment. "Ok. Yeah. Maybe you're right. And if we went ahead and started an agency, would you join us, Alan?" he asked.

When I walked into the apartment just after 7 o'clock, the kids were screaming, toys were strewn all over the living room, and Wendy, worn out, was trying to get dinner started. Heidi was four, Lee was one, and our cramped place was feeling smaller by the day.

I told her that Marvin, Len, and I were thinking of starting our own agency.

My timing wasn't great for this announcement. But Wendy sat on the couch with me, Lee on her lap, and listened. She asked questions and shared my excitement. She didn't ask how we'd be able to swing it, and neither of us looked at the glass jar of spare change sitting on top of the bookshelf—our savings for the occasional dinner out and a babysitter. It wasn't the first time (nor would it be the last) that I realized how lucky I was that this incredible woman had agreed to marry me.

I had been at PKL for a few years. Right out of business school, I had cut my teeth in marketing as a product manager at Standard Brands, a consumer products company. One of my roles as a product manager was to work with our ad agency, Ted Bates, to promote my brands, Blue Bonnet Margarine and Royal Desserts. My agency contact was a debonair fellow who took me out for fancy lunches (a nice change from the Standard Brands cafeteria) and invited me to a NY Giants home game, where the agency had box seats. For a 27-year-old just out of grad school, these perks felt like the "big time."

Yes, the advertising business was glamorous, but what really appealed to me was that it seemed to be in the thick of things at an exciting and turbulent time. Today, we talk about the sixties as a decade of great change, a description that doesn't come close to conveying what it *felt* like. It was rattling, exhilarating, terrifying, and inspiring—all at the same time. For me, it began with euphoria and idealism when Kennedy took office, the youngest president we'd ever elected (and the first Catholic). He exhorted us to be better, to live up to our highest ideals. As historian Alan Brinkley so aptly put it, JFK made us believe that together we could solve hard problems and accomplish bold deeds.[21] I was bowled over by the elegance, optimism, and energy of this young man. His words and deeds gave me aspirations to reach beyond my immediate world, to think bigger.

But we also found ourselves in a Cold War, and we worried about the Bomb. We were swept off our feet by the Beatles. Bewitched by Marilyn Monroe. One day we turned on the news to hear that our president had been shot, the footage and horror permanently seared into our memories. We placed our hopes for civil rights in LBJ and Dr. Martin Luther King, as the KKK ramped up its racist campaign of terror and intimidation. Then we got the Civil Rights Act in 1964, hallelujah! Then, more killings by the KKK. And Bloody Sunday, when Alabama state troopers beat peaceful demonstrators marching for Black voting rights. Then the war that wasn't technically a war hit home in '65 with the draft. More than 2,000 service members had already been killed in Vietnam, and we had no way of knowing how many more Americans and Vietnamese civilians would die. If only we'd paid more attention to the thousands of protesters who took to the streets of New York and gathered with their signs at the United Nations, just a few blocks from Madison Avenue. Most of them, young students stepping forward to protest. *Stop. This is wrong.*

And that was just the first half of the decade.

The nation's collective yearning, confusion, anger, and idealism found expression in its advertising, which became edgy, rebellious, and hard-hitting. Like the nation, advertising was in flux and recasting itself, too. Ads not only reflected the changes their creators observed in the world around them, but they also contributed to the changes.

It was a dramatic shift from advertising in the '50s, when ads were wholesome, rosy, and congenial. Celebratory of all things American and grand. GM sold cars with the "See the USA in your Chevrolet!" an upbeat jingle sung by Dinah Shore. Cars kept getting bigger, their fins longer and engines more powerful. Our nation had been on a sugar high of consumption since the end of the war. Bigger was better. Like cars, ads in the '50s were big, colorful, and splashy.

In 1959, a small agency by the name of Doyle Dane Bernbach (DDB) came out with a campaign for the Volkswagen Beetle that challenged the American notion of big. "Think small," said the quiet headline that would send tremors through the advertising industry. It was a stark ad, most of it white space. A small, odd-looking car floated on the left side of the page. At the bottom, a bit of copy talked about everything that Chevrolet *wasn't* without mentioning Chevrolet. This car was German, and "German-made" was still a sensitive subject 13 years after the war. The Beetle was also small, uncomfortable, inexpensive, and would last for years. Not to worry, though, because next year's model would look exactly the same.

The campaign, created by Helmut Krone under the direction of Bill Bernbach, was honest, witty, self-deprecating, and eye-catching. It broke most of the rules of conventional advertising. And it sold cars. Lots of them. With the iconic Volkswagen campaign, DDB precipitated a creative revolution, ushering in what became known as the Golden Age of advertising.

By the time I was looking to enter the industry, Bernbach's philosophy and approach had caught on. Creativity had exploded, and the best ads made you do a double-take with their wry irreverence. Ads were no longer meant to reassure and make us feel good. They challenged and went right to the point, reflecting the turbulent and questioning mood of the country. Advertising played a visible role in politics. One of the commercials used in LBJ's 1964 reelection campaign against Barry Goldwater (created by DDB in partnership with Tony Schwartz, a sound designer and media consultant) showed a little blonde girl plucking petals off a daisy, with the countdown ending in a mushroom cloud (the implication: this is what will happen if we elect Goldwater). It was a sledgehammer approach that would have been unthinkable a few years earlier.

It wasn't just the script that had changed; the players were different, too. No longer the domain of a handful of staid, privately held firms controlled largely by the pedigreed elite from the "right" families and the "best" schools, advertising now attracted young men and women of diverse educational and ethnic backgrounds. Agencies that were going public got bigger, while small, dynamic shops continued to crop up and make their mark with fresh, creative talent and ads that crackled with wit. The "Mad Men" series captured some of the frenetic energy and freewheeling culture of the era, but it missed the burgeoning role of women. Some of the best copywriters of the late '50s and '60s were women. Mary Wells Lawrence, who spent her early career at McCann Erikson and DDB (among others), started her own agency, Wells Rich Greene, the year before we opened our agency. Fiercely talented, she became a major force in the industry and was the first female CEO of a company listed on the New York Stock Exchange.[22]

All this was irresistible to me. I jumped at the opportunity to participate in an industry reinventing itself, and I was fortunate to land at PKL when it was at the peak of its influence and considered by many to be the creative successor to DDB. Now three years into it, I was contemplating leaving a good job with a nice salary, where I was the supervisor of the exalted Proctor & Gamble account. My future at PKL was looking bright. Yet I was itching for more. My conversation on Third Avenue with Marvin and Len in 1966 came at the right time.

"WHY TAKE THE risk?" my father-in-law asked Marvin and me over lunch. Milton Stern was an accomplished marketing consultant, and he knew the New York advertising industry well. "You'll be just another small agency operating on the fringes," Milton warned. I'd been hoping for his suggestions and ideas on *how* we might proceed—not *whether* we should. The more he tried to talk me out of it, the more I dug in my heels.

Milton didn't need to point out that I had a growing family to support. Wendy and I were expecting our third child, so perhaps it wasn't the ideal time for me to take such a risk. On the other hand, the world was showing me what was possible. Young men and women were challenging convention and old-world thinking, precipitating changes in society, business, and politics. Why not me, too? I was confident that Marvin, Len, and I could pull it off. Most important, Wendy believed in me.

There was no question of starting a new business without her support. From the first day of our marriage, Wendy and I were able to face big decisions together and without contention. And in the 60 years since, that hasn't changed. While I am most often the instigator of change, Wendy is no pushover. Her shy and reserved demeanor can be misleading. When we met, she was twenty years old, beautiful, gentle, and fun. I had no idea that this demure girl, a full head shorter than I, was a fantastic, fearless skier. Nor could I have imagined how much tougher Wendy would become, physically and emotionally, as our years together unfolded. My wife is still beautiful, gentle, and fun. And she can still leave most skiers behind in a cloud of powder.

Wendy is like a stealth bomber flying under the radar: when she arrives, she blows you away with her calm strength, determination, and unerring moral compass. Early in my SMS career, I occasionally found myself swept up in the prestige and trappings of my profession. At a dinner one evening with friends, I was feeling quite pleased with myself, and I pulled a cigar out of my pocket. Before I could light it, Wendy gently plucked the cigar out of my mouth and broke it in half. Smiling, she said, "To tell you the truth, I hate those things," and then continued her conversation with the dinner guest on her right. I loved it. I detest the image of the self-satisfied, cigar-smoking man high on his success. Wendy called me on it.

Wendy has been game for virtually all my crazy schemes and adventures. But she won't hesitate to put her foot down when I get out of line. She was so pissed at me once about the weekend hours I spent on the tennis court when I should have been spending more time with the family that she threw a dish with enough force to send shards scattering through the kitchen. (Fortunately, she threw the plate on the floor and not at me. Her aim is excellent.) But when it came to putting every penny of our savings into a start-up business, Wendy's belief was unwavering. She trusted me.

I DON'T LABOR over things. I never have. If I think something makes sense or feels right, I'll do it. If I screw up, or if something doesn't work out, I put it into a little compartment, throw the compartment overboard, hopefully learn from it, and then I move on. Sure, I've made my share of mistakes, but, for the most part, acting on gut instinct and jumping in with both feet have led to great adventures and invaluable learning experiences.

When I was halfway through college, I decided to extend my ROTC commitment beyond the required two years. At the time, ROTC (Reserve Officer Training Corp) was mandatory for all young men attending college or university; at the end of the two years, you could opt out, which is what most people did, or you could commit to another two years. I wish I could say I was motivated by a sense of duty to my country, but the truth is I thought that serving in the military after college might be interesting and challenging. An adventure. Why not? The timing turned out to be lucky: the Korean War ended shortly after I made my commitment, and the US didn't send its first combat troops to Vietnam until after I was out of the military.

I reported to Fort Benning in Georgia for the Basic Infantry Officers Course (BIOC) as a newly commissioned Second Lieutenant shortly after graduation. The evening after I arrived, my roommate, a few other new arrivals, and I drove into Columbus, the closest town to Fort Benning. Columbus—a city of about 100,000 in 1956—seemed like a different world to those of us visiting the South for the first time. As we approached the city center, traffic slowed to a crawl around a brightly lit stadium where a policeman was directing traffic. We pulled alongside him, and I rolled down my window to ask if there was a football game in the stadium, thinking maybe we should get tickets.

"Nah," the White cop said. "Just a bunch of n-----s knocking heads."

I rolled up my window and turned to look at my new buddies. I didn't know what to say. I had witnessed racism in the Northeast, but it was more subtle there. In Georgia, it was jarring—unvarnished and unapologetic. You couldn't get away from it. Everything was segregated in 1956—bathrooms, water fountains, buses, schools, hospitals, lunch counters. But segregation in the military had officially ended in 1948, when President Truman signed the executive order outlawing racial segregation in the US Armed Forces. Within the gates of Fort Benning, all the men in our BIOC group were equal by law, if not always in practice. On base, Black soldiers and White soldiers trained and socialized together. Once we left the base, it was another story. In Columbus, we couldn't have lunch together. It would be another eight years before President Johnson signed the Civil Rights Act, prohibiting segregation in public places and banning employment discrimination.

The Northeast had *seemed* more progressive to me, but systemic discrimination was still very much in place there, as well. It was just packaged more discreetly. Many elite colleges, for example, had unofficial admission quotas based on race and religion. There was only a handful of African American students at Lafayette College when I was there. My fraternity was one of only two that welcomed Jews. When I attended The Tuck School at Dartmouth College for my MBA, there wasn't a single student of color in my class. And there were no women.

I realize now how privileged I was to be a White male. But as Jews, Herb and I were not exempt from racial hostility in the military. In our barracks, a few of the rooms above ours were occupied by Citadel graduates. Most of them appeared to be football players. One night, when Herb and I were hanging out in our room, they began blasting on their record player *Deutschland über Alles*, the German national anthem, which had been perverted and co-opted by the Nazis during the war.

"Hey, you guys down there," the Citadel graduates shouted. "If y'all don't like the music, wanna come upstairs and tell us what you're gonna do about it?"

I could not reconcile their anti-Semitism with the photos I'd seen of American service members liberating Holocaust survivors from concentration camps eleven years before. But I should not have been surprised. Racism is wily and capricious. When American officers and soldiers were liberating Jews and helping to restore democracy in a decimated Germany, the US military still operated under the same Jim Crow laws that codified segregation and discrimination back home. A recent *New York Times* article reminded me that African American service members, essential to the war effort, were treated as second-class citizens by their fellow soldiers, even as they mingled freely with German citizens, who couldn't understand why Black soldiers were segregated from their White compatriots.[23]

After completing BIOC, I received orders to report to Fort Dix, New Jersey, as an instructor for recruits going through basic training. In hindsight, it seems preposterous that I was put in charge of two of the most dangerous ranges that recruits had to navigate in basic training: first, the infiltration course, and then the hand grenade range. I was 23, with only six months of training.

My task as officer in charge at the hand grenade range was to supervise fifteen sergeants who, in turn, oversaw two hundred recruits as they learned how to throw live hand grenades. In the infiltration course, recruits had to crawl on their bellies under barbed wire with bullets zinging over their heads. Somehow, at the time, it didn't terrify me. It does now. Anything could have gone wrong. A recruit might have panicked and dropped a live hand grenade. A bullet could have ricocheted and hit a crawling recruit. It was the first time I was responsible for the lives of other people. Though I underestimated the hazards, the gravity of that responsibility left a strong imprint, tempering my confidence with a dose of humility.

AT FORT DIX I met a fellow officer who'd been to business school—the Amos Tuck School at Dartmouth. I'd never heard of the school, nor, for that matter, of a graduate business degree. But it sounded far more interesting to me than law school, the route I'd chosen more or less by default. My idea of becoming a doctor fizzled out in freshman year when I took chemistry. In truth, I wasn't so much fixed on a particular profession as I was on finding a way to make a bigger life.

When I was a kid in Queens, my friends and I would walk to Cunningham Park and sit on a grassy hill overlooking Union Turnpike, a major thoroughfare. We'd watch the cars go by, eager to spot our favorite models, the ones we hoped to drive one day: maybe a Pontiac coupe, a Chrysler convertible, or a Hudson Commodore. Those cars represented another world to me. Once I got my driver's license, I'd borrow my dad's car, drive to Great Neck and Roslyn, and look longingly at the large houses with sweeping lawns and stately trees. Homes on *properties*. Our house was on a small lot in a planned community. Which is not to say that our neighborhood wasn't nice, but the houses on our street looked pretty much the same and were crammed together.

Back then, my idea of "more" represented something concrete and material—things I could see for myself that were different, bigger, or better than what my parents had. In high school, I looked for athletic achievement and a diverse group of friends. As I got older, "more" meant new experiences—like traveling to another country. In the service, I was able to hitch a free plane ride on a military transport to Europe. When I finally got to France, one of the first things I did was go to the Paris opera. I knew next to nothing about opera, but I wanted to experience it for myself. I loved it.

The chance conversation with my fellow officer about business schools led to an abrupt change in plans. I decided to forgo my acceptance at Georgetown Law School and apply to two business schools instead. One accepted me. It wasn't a brilliant academic record or stellar test scores that got me in. What tipped the scales in my favor had more to do with a snowstorm, stubbornness, and a bit of luck.

My interview at the Tuck School was scheduled for a Saturday in February, and I would have to drive to New Hampshire from Fort Dix. Under normal circumstances, the drive should have taken 8 to10 hours. Unfortunately, a big snowstorm hit New England a few hours after I left Fort Dix, and my 10-hour drive became a harrowing 18-hour odyssey. I finally straggled into White River Junction, Vermont, at around midnight and was lucky to find a motel. My appointment with Dean Karl Hill was scheduled for 9 a.m. the next day. I wasn't looking forward to the six-mile drive from White River over the state line to Hanover, New Hampshire, on a winding two-lane country road with two feet of fresh snow. Luck was with me. The road was slick, but at least it had been plowed.

When I arrived, the school seemed deserted. I had to wade through knee-high snow to get to the front door of Tuck Hall. I was beginning to doubt whether anyone would even be there. *Great*, I thought. *I've come all this way, and my interview is probably canceled.* I was relieved to find the door open and sat down to wait in a dark-paneled room furnished with formal leather chairs and sporting prints. Everything looked very "Ivy League" to me (or, at least, what I'd imagined "Ivy" might look like). I was intimidated.

I hadn't bothered applying to Ivy League schools for college. My high school grades were not good enough, and I was a Jewish kid from a working-class family in Queens. I looked around the room uncomfortably. My shoes were soaked, my toes felt like ice blocks, and the blue suit I was so pleased with earlier that morning was now damp. The neat creases I had carefully ironed were gone.

I was bent over, pulling the wet pant legs away from my ankles, when the door blew open. A tall man walked in trailing snow. His pants were wisely tucked into a sturdy pair of LL Bean boots; the rest of him was hidden under a thick duffel coat, woolen hat, and plaid scarf. The only part of him I could see were his eyes, which looked at me with surprise.

"Are you Alan?" he asked.

I nodded. "I am."

"Looks like we're the only people here today. Come on in," he said and gestured to his office.

He pulled out my application and GMAT scores—both of which he'd already reviewed. Dean Hill was friendly and approachable, and we had a great conversation. Then he said, "You've got a strong résumé, and your letters of recommendation are impressive. You have everything we like to see in our candidates. Except for your GMAT test scores. Sorry, but they're too low."

I wasn't surprised. I took the GMATs twice and managed to do slightly worse the second time around.

"But, on the other hand," he said, pointing to the whirl of snow outside his window, "you're here. In spite of the snowstorm. I'm just curious—why didn't you call to postpone and reschedule your interview like everyone else on my calendar today?"

"Honestly, it never crossed my mind," I said. "The interview was scheduled, and I want to get into this school." (I didn't mention that the only other school I applied to had already rejected me.)

The interview ended with the Dean telling me he had reason enough to deny me admission. But due to my sheer doggedness in driving almost 400 miles, much of it through a blinding snowstorm, he was going to recommend the school take a chance on me.

It was one of the most important lessons I took away from business school. You may not always succeed, but you *will* miss every shot you don't take. And it's impossible to project what might evolve from the chances you do take. Neither the Dean nor I could have envisioned that my acceptance "by a hair" would decades later lead to an unusual bond between the Tuck School and my family. Not because our son Greg would also attend the school, or because of my years serving as overseer (akin to a trustee) and as an executive in residence. But because of Lee. Shortly after we opened our doors, the Lee Pesky Learning Center became the subject of a case study that is still used at the school today. Each year when I'm invited to speak at Tuck, it's because the students want to hear the story of Lee and the founding of the nonprofit that bears his name and the profound impact he and the Center have had on my life.

THE DAY AFTER Marvin, Len, and I agreed to start our agency, a stark realization set in. We had no copywriter and no art director. Holy shit—what were we thinking? Len was in research, and Marvin and I both worked on the marketing side, in account management. Opening an agency without a copywriter and an art director would be like opening a restaurant without a chef.

Marvin suggested we talk to Sam Scali, who was an art director at PKL. "I have a good relationship with Sam and can speak with him confidentially," Marvin assured us. "He knows a lot of the creative people at different agencies in New York, and he might be able to recommend someone."

He visited Sam, and, to Marvin's surprise, Sam recommended himself. I didn't know Sam well, but he had a good reputation at PKL. We now only had one crucial role to fill. We needed a copywriter who could collaborate with Sam to produce great advertising.

Sam knew a young copywriter doing some exciting work at the Carl Ally agency. "He's a few years younger than we are," Sam said. "Brash and very, very good." His name was Ed McCabe.

After he met with Ed, Marvin reported back to us. "He's an obnoxious, arrogant little guy, but he writes damn good ads. And he's interested. He wants to meet with you, Alan."

My first meeting with Ed was like a fencing match. He grilled me about my experience as an account executive; I responded, parried, and, in turn, prodded him. Creative talent is arguably the single most important component of advertising. Nevertheless, account management—the area of the agency I would be heading—develops the overall marketing strategy that establishes the framework for all the creative work. Account managers are responsible for shepherding the creative end product through the delicate client-agency dance. I knew Ed wouldn't agree to join us unless he could be assured that his work would be well received by clients and that it would get the exposure it deserved.

I passed his test. We had our fifth partner, and we were ready to move ahead.

Marvin Sloves was the only one of my soon-to-be partners whom I knew well. Shortly after I joined PKL, I was assigned the cubicle next to Marvin's. I had just hung up the phone after a very animated conversation with one of our art directors when Marvin popped his head over the partition.

"You have to do me a favor," he said. "Can you please modulate your conversation? You have a very loud voice. I'm trying to write something, and your yelling is making it hard for me to concentrate."

"I'm very sorry," I said with a straight face, "I talk loudly because I'm a bit hard of hearing."

Marvin looked mortified and said, "Oh my God, I am so sorry, I didn't realize that."

He must have seen the start of a grin at the corners of my mouth, because we both burst out laughing. It was an off-color wisecrack I wouldn't think about making today. But Marvin and I remember it vividly, cringing now about some of the things we said fifty years ago.

Marvin was charming, charismatic, and smart. Like me, he was ambitious. Only a few months apart in age, we came from similar backgrounds. We both had strong opinions and were not shy about defending them. Marvin and I argued a lot.

One of our more explosive discussions took place on Lexington Avenue in front of a shoe store. We had just landed the Stride Rite Shoe account, and Marvin and I were walking around looking for shoe stores to chat with people about Stride Rite shoes. Before we even opened the door to the first store, we got into a shouting match on the sidewalk. People inside the store stared at us through the window, mouths open, while pedestrians made a cautious detour around us.

Then, like a summer storm, the argument was over. One of us laughed at the other and said, "What are we arguing about? Shoes?" And that was it. Marvin and I would disagree, we'd fight, and then we'd forget about it.

Years later, neither of us can remember what exactly we fought over—just that we did. And that we sometimes brought the people around us to tears (not the laughing kind). A bit like brothers, I suppose.

Now Marvin and I were in partnership with three other people. Five equal partners who had virtually nothing in common other than the desire to produce great advertising and to make a lot of money. All in our early 30s, we were not quite as poor as church mice, but darned close. Len, Marvin, and I scraped together enough money to get the agency off the ground. Neither Ed nor Sam had a dime, so their investment came in the form of creative talent.

We agreed to manage the agency as a team, our specific roles reflecting our respective strengths. The public face of our new agency had to be someone suave and savvy—an adept salesman. That person was, without question, Marvin Sloves, who would be our president. Sam and Ed were V.P.s of our creative departments. My role as executive V.P. would be to head up marketing and client services, which was well suited to my experience and temperament. And Len Hultgren would take on research, operations, and finance.

We couldn't have been more different in temperament or background: Sam was wiry and steady, ruthless in his demand for creative excellence; Len was reserved, precise, and played chess at lunch; Ed, the only one of us who didn't go to college, was brilliant, pugnacious, and (in the words of Paula Span of the *Washington Post*) "a tireless self-promotor"; and Marvin, a former University of Chicago graduate student of Chinese literature, was stylish and canny.[24] Our coming together as partners was somewhat random. Together, we were able to create magic, yet we weren't close friends. Some of us didn't even particularly like each other. (I once tried to throw a phone at Ed because I was so pissed at him.)

All four of my partners were talented and essential to the partnership and our success. But Marvin is the one I find myself thinking about the most. He became a sort of father figure and "shrink" to our employees. He was incapable of firing anyone. (He left that to me.) Marvin could charm even our most macho clients. Most days, he would arrive at the office with an expensive overcoat draped over his shoulders and a Borsalino fedora tipped at just the right angle. You never would have guessed that Marvin was the son of a boxer—Johnny Murray, a.k.a. "The Bronx Bone Crusher." Marvin also happened to be gay. He and I never talked about it, but the sixties, seventies, and eighties were not a safe time to come out. In a moment of unusual candor, when I was telling him about my latest adventure trip, Marvin confided to me, "Alan, you're the son my father always wanted."

What a strange irony. I'd gripe to myself about my father because he didn't live up to *my* expectations, and Marvin thought he was a disappointment to his father, "the bone crusher," whom he idolized. Boxing photos and memorabilia of Johnny Murray's glory days in the ring adorned Marvin's office on Madison Avenue.

I've often wondered how excruciating the decades-long concealment must have been for Marvin and so many others. To love someone in secret. It wasn't until Marvin was in his early eighties that he was able to marry his partner of more than thirty years.

OUR FIRST FEW days in our starter office at the Gotham Hotel felt like weeks. But it wasn't long before we acquired our first client, albeit a nonpaying one. Citizens for a Quieter City (CQC), a nonprofit, was referred to us by a friend of a friend of Marvin's. John Wharton, a board member of CQC, was a principal of the law firm Paul, Weiss, Rifkind, Wharton & Garrison. John agreed to have one of the partners handle our incorporation gratis if we, in turn, would take care of CQC's marketing needs. It was a start. And John Wharton did us another good turn. He was able to get us a photo shoot with Richard Avedon for our agency brochure. Avedon, who was already a celebrated photographer, was very gracious as he "shot" us, even as he must have been wondering who the hell we were.

While we were doing our part to make New York a quieter city, we learned that Volvo was looking for a new US agency. They'd had a falling out with their agency, Carl Ally—not an unusual occurrence in an industry of big egos. Volvo was familiar with Ed's work from his time at Carl Ally, and word got to us that they wanted to go with a small shop—one that was creative and hungry. Ed gave them a call, and we were soon in the running along with five other agencies.

A few weeks later, the Volvo account was awarded to Scali, McCabe, Sloves, and it was reported to be the largest piece of business ever to go to a brand-new agency that had started with no clients. It was an incredible stroke of fortune for us, and it instantly put our bare-bones agency on the map. More clients followed, and two months after our opening we were able to move out of our two-room space at the Gotham Hotel into slick new offices at 635 Madison Avenue. By the end of the year, we had 25 employees and billings of $7 million. Eight years later, in 1975, Scali, McCabe, Sloves was named Agency of the Year by *Advertising Age*, the industry "bible." It was only the second year the award was given, and SMS was the smallest agency ever to be so honored. The following year, we were the subject of the *New York Times Magazine* cover story, "New! Improved! Advertising!" featuring a visual from one of our ads— Uncle Sam eyeballing a Hebrew National hotdog.[25] A year later, Ogilvy & Mather, a prestigious international agency, called us. Would we be interested in selling our agency to them?

It was 1977. I was 44 years old and nearing the pinnacle of my career after a 15-year blur that had, at times, felt like a rocket ride. Heidi, our eldest child, was 15 years old, and Greg, the youngest, was nine. They were thriving in every possible way. Lee was thirteen, and his learning disabilities and motor challenges were becoming more apparent as they collided with my expectations. The more I accomplished, the greater my expectations became and the less patient I was with Lee, who was nearing the halfway point in his life.

WITH SCALI, MCCABE, SLOVES, I had achieved financial security for myself and my family, something I had always hoped for. Perhaps it was important to me because I was born during the Depression and had a father who gambled. Yet once I had money, I found little satisfaction in acquiring *stuff*. Yes, we were able to buy a beautiful home in the suburbs, and I did get a brief thrill from having a Porsche as my company car for a year. But at the end of the day, a car is just a car: a way to get you from point A to point B. For most of my life, I've owned boring cars and have kept them for a long time. I've worn the same watch for 45 years—a gift from Wendy for our fifteenth anniversary.

Most of all, money allowed me to have new experiences, to challenge myself through outdoor adventure. Every one of these trips delighted and enriched me, even those that didn't quite go as planned. The notorious 75-kilometer Finlancia-hiihto cross-country ski marathon, which I approached somewhat lightheartedly, seemed like a good idea at the time. But I was woefully unprepared for the brutally cold conditions and was plucked off the course after eight hours, only two-thirds of the way through, with severe frostbite.

Wendy and I traveled a lot together. Our most outlandish adventure was inspired by my reading of *From Alice to the Ocean*, Robyn Davidson's book about her journey on camelback across the Australian Outback. I was determined to recreate the experience on a tandem bike with Wendy. She thought I was nuts, but she humored me. It was an incredible, blistering, and dusty experience.

Some of our accommodations on these trips didn't thrill Wendy. A hotel in Vietnam comes to mind. It was on our cycling trip in 1995, and the country was still rebuilding itself following the war. The hotel looked fine from the outside, but when we walked up the stairs from the lobby, we could see patches of gray sky through the gaping holes left by bombs. The shower spigot in our bathroom was a rubber hose positioned over a hole in the floor, which also doubled as the toilet. Cobwebs hung everywhere in the room, and when I went to the window to pull back the threadbare curtains, I found the spider. It was about the size of my fist. I screamed and jumped back landing next to Wendy, who was sitting on the bed looking around in disbelief. She turned to me and said, "After a day of riding 60 miles in the rain, I just need to get the fuck out of here."

I pride myself on being a pretty quick thinker. "Wait here," I said. "I'll be right back." I ran downstairs. Cycling through town, we had passed dozens of vendors selling everything from souvenirs to Scotch whisky. I bought a bottle of Johnny Walker Red from the street vendor next to the hotel and ran back upstairs. Wendy and I have been fortunate to share many experiences as a couple, some more unexpected than others. That night, Wendy and I sat on the bed and knocked off most of the Scotch.

Perhaps the most meaningful vacations we took were our family adventure trips. The first was a two-week river trip through the Grand Canyon in 1974, well before Grand Canyon float trips became commonplace. A couple of years later, we went on a five-day winter camping and ski-trekking trip in the Sawtooth Mountains of Idaho. After that, there were rafting trips on the middle fork of the Salmon River. What stands out for me now is how the five of us were able to connect with one another in a way we didn't at home. Lee and I always got along well on these trips. He had a wonderful time and managed the physical rigors and challenges as well as any of us.

Nature is an equalizer. The wilderness, the mountains, and the rivers don't care how good your tennis game is. They are indifferent to your accomplishments. We left our "stories" and expectations behind every time we ventured into a wild place. Lee could be Lee in an environment where he was unencumbered by learning challenges, unconstrained by the expectations of others.

Skiing together was another matter. In the '70s, we were able to buy a vacation condo in Sun Valley, Idaho, where we would hike in the summer and ski in the winter. We always skied in a large family group, usually for five or six hours at a stretch. I didn't want to waste time waiting in line for lunch in the mountain lodge, so we'd bring along sandwiches, stop for a 30-minute break on one of the lodge terraces, and then continue skiing. We skied the hard stuff—off-trail terrain and black diamond slopes. One of my friends in Sun Valley rolled her eyes when I recently told her about our take-no-prisoners approach to skiing. "I would have hated skiing with you, Alan," she said. "Hated it. That's not my idea of fun."

It wasn't Lee's, either.

"We're all going together, and we're leaving at 8:30 for first tracks," I'd yell from the foot of the stairs the morning after a big dump of snow. "Don't be late. We're meeting your aunt and uncle and cousins on the mountain."

Lee and his cousin Mark would find any excuse not to go up with us or to delay our departure. Just as we'd be ready to leave the house, Lee's goggles or a glove would go missing. Or his ski pass would be lost under a pile of clothes in his room. Or he might have a stomachache. At a young age, Heidi and Greg were already jumping off moguls. I was maniacal, usually the fastest one down the mountain. We were a tough crowd. I sucked the air out of the room with everything I wanted to do.

You can exhort your kids to achieve, but decency is not something you can teach with words. You can only model it, and I believe Wendy and I did so in many meaningful ways. When our kids were young, though, I made sure they knew how important it was to me that they showed ambition and strove for excellence. Not only did I commemorate Lee's first hockey goal by framing his puck, I did something similar for Heidi. When she and I won a father-daughter tennis tournament, I framed that award, too. I was the "overachieving Alan" in that phase of my life. A bit of an asshole, perhaps.

When Lee and I were butting heads, it never occurred to me that he might not be the problem. Wendy and I hadn't made the connection between his behavior and the frustration he was experiencing as a result of his learning and motor challenges. I realize now that instead of taking Lee to a psychiatrist when he was a kid, we should have been the ones to seek help. Especially me.

For years, we asked the wrong question: How can we solve *Lee's* problem? An understandable reaction for parents. But now we know enough to ask better ones: *What kind of challenges is Lee dealing with? What can we do to help him thrive?* Today, a learning specialist would reassure us that our son is a great kid who is simply frustrated because he's got some processing challenges that manifest in certain ways—among them, behavioral issues. We would be told that, in the right environment and with the right guidance, our son *can* be a successful learner. And that he will come to enjoy certain sports. A psychologist would tell me to relax. Not to yell at my son to get up early in the morning to get out on the slopes because I love to ski and expect him to love it, as well.

Eventually, Lee did embrace skiing. He became passionate about it in spite of my relentless pushing—but only once he could do it on his terms. Our children shouldn't have to replicate our dreams, our successes, or our stories. They are entitled to their own dreams and how to realize them. Joan Didion said something to the effect that being a teenager is hard enough, let alone being expected to do it with someone else's script.[26]

When I speak of our kids today, it is not a scorecard of accomplishments I extol. I am most proud of them for who they are: great parents, loving partners, and happy, fulfilled individuals who are generous and actively involved with their communities. Heidi, Lee, and Greg are very different from one another, but the one thing they all have in common is a core of goodness. They always treated other people well. All three, great human beings.

LEE CHOSE TO settle in Ketchum because he understood, well before I did, what was important for him. He realized he could thrive in an environment in which the things he struggled with didn't matter. Where he could be himself. That's why we chose to have Lee buried in the cemetery in Ketchum, Idaho.

Lee lies a stone's throw from Ernest Hemingway's grave. When I hear the words from Ecclesiastes that inspired the title of one of Hemingway's most famous books, *The sun also rises, and the sun goes down and hastens to the place where it arose,* I think of Lee in Idaho, where amongst the mountains and stars my son camps forever.

WHENEVER I ARRIVE in Sun Valley, and before I leave, I visit Lee. I place a stone on top of his craggy, mountain-shaped tombstone. It is a tradition in the Jewish faith to place a stone on a gravesite when you visit. I don't know the origin of the practice nor its significance, but I like it. I let the stones be a sign of my love, and I keep adding to the ever-growing pile.

Chapter 10

The Measure of One's Life

"I've concluded that the metric by which God will assess my life isn't dollars but the individual people whose lives I've touched."
—Clayton M. Christensen, Harvard Business School professor, author of *How Will You Measure Your Life?*[27]

"Gentlemen. You. Are. Pigs," Jock Elliott, Chairman of Ogilvy & Mather, said.

He and Andrew Kershaw, titans of the international advertising world, were not amused. Next to me, Marvin shifted uncomfortably in his chair. The servers hovering nearby backed off, and the Four Seasons restaurant suddenly seemed quieter. I wasn't sure how to respond. Grin and laugh it off? Tell them we were just kidding?

A few weeks before, Ogilvy & Mather had agreed to buy our agency for an incredible amount of money. The purpose of our lunch meeting with Elliott and Kershaw was to discuss the final detail of our deal: retirement benefits for the five Scali, McCabe, Sloves partners. Marvin, Ed, Sam, and I had contracts to stay on with Ogilvy post-acquisition; Len would be moving on to pursue his passion for wine in Napa Valley.

The lunch had started off cordially, with firm handshakes and restrained backslapping. Innocuous small talk occupied us through most of the meal. When the table was cleared and coffee had been served, Jock

Elliot got down to business. "Have you given further thought to your retirement packages?"

Marvin looked at me.

"Yes," I said, "we have talked it over." I paused. "We would like to receive the same retirement package as David Ogilvy."

Silence. Then Jock's icy pronouncement: We were pigs.

Jock's face was stone. I could imagine the outraged thoughts behind his words. *How dare these New York advertising upstarts presume to put themselves on a level with David Ogilvy?* Ogilvy, founder of the storied firm that would be acquiring us, was known in the industry as "The Father of Advertising." He was a godlike figure to the men sitting across the table from us.

Was it absurd? A ballsy thing to ask for? Absolutely. In the end, we did get very nice pensions, though not the equivalent of David Ogilvy's. But why not ask?

THE "PIG CONVERSATION" marked what would be the beginning of the end of a major chapter in my life. At the time, asking for even more on top of an already dazzling price for our agency didn't feel greedy to me. Not too many years before, my partners and I might indeed have been considered "upstarts." But that day at lunch in 1977, Jock Elliott's put-down aside, we were on top of the world. We were the founders and owners of one of the hottest shops on Madison Avenue. And out of all the independent advertising agencies in New York, Ogilvy & Mather wanted *us*.

Our world became even more glamorous after we joined Ogilvy & Mather. Before SMS, I had only been on a few international flights. Now I was traveling all over the world, flying first-class. Taking the Concorde to London and Paris. Attending board meetings in Venice. And we were getting bigger. As president of SMS International, I was tasked with acquiring hot, creative agencies around the world, just as we had been acquired. Within four years, we had offices in London, Mexico City, Duesseldorf, Sydney, Paris, and Toronto, and in two more US cities. I was engaged in an exalted game of Pac-Man, with the goal of expanding Ogilvy & Mather's empire so that they (and we) could make more money. It was heady and exciting. For a while it was gratifying. Fun, too. Until it wasn't. Being on a plane a few times a month got old fast. I would make a point of going for a run as soon as I arrived in whichever city it was that week. Running helped keep me grounded, and it was a good way to get to know a new city. But nothing could make up for the time I was away from my family.

What's more, SMS was losing its creative verve. Initially, we operated as an independently managed entity under the Ogilvy umbrella: they agreed not to tell us what to do, how to manage our accounts, or what kind of ads to create—as long as we produced. But as part of a large, multinational public company driven by shareholder value, SMS came under tremendous pressure to grow. The values driving our business changed. Simply put, the game was no longer about creating the best advertising; it was about getting bigger. And the bigger we got, the more we attracted larger corporate clients—like Hertz, Pepsi, and Nikon—and the harder it became to do the kind of great advertising that is born of a tight-knit, almost familial, client-agency relationship. Major corporations were, for the most part, rule followers; even though they were attracted by our edginess and creative energy, they tended to be risk-averse when it came to their advertising.

The goal of advertising is to sell. But for me, the *magic* of advertising lies in sparking connections and shifting perspectives. It's less about products than about people and their emotions, perceptions of value, and aspirations. An agency's job is to find a way to forge a relationship between brand and consumer—ideally, by building trust. The young SMS flourished at a time when advertising was designed to touch a nerve by *not* following the rules. And I loved that about our work.

SMS's early momentum was a testimony to our insistence on creative excellence, focus on building strong relationships, and willingness to defy convention. We had many talented women and men on our team who poured their passion into their work and took risks with their ideas. We had clients who inspired us with their dedication to quality and who were willing to take risks in how they presented themselves to the world. Clients like Volvo, Hebrew National, and Barneys trusted us to address perceived marketing liabilities head-on and turn them into strengths. The boxiness of Volvos became associated with safety and durability. The "kosherness" of Hebrew National hotdogs became synonymous with quality ("We answer to a higher authority"). Barneys's out-of-the-way location became proof that it was worth the detour. Changing the narrative about a company or a product with a few well-chosen words and a simple visual was not only challenging, it was also fun. And no account was more unusual, more critical to the rapid rise of our start-up agency, than Perdue Farms.

Frank Perdue's story exemplified the groundbreaking spirit of the era. He had transformed his father's egg farm into a multimillion-dollar chicken processor without spending a dime on advertising. At the time, consumers didn't think about the name on the package of chicken they picked up at the supermarket. A chicken was a chicken was a chicken—a commodity. But Frank Perdue believed he could do better, so in 1970, he set himself a modest advertising budget of $250,000 (chicken feed, even in those days) and went shopping for an agency.

Frank approached his search with the determination of a military commander and the subtlety of a battering ram. He interviewed more than 50 agencies—probably the largest search ever conducted for such a small account. Small, but highly coveted, because no one had ever advertised chickens before. It was irresistible, and just about everyone in the business wanted a crack at the Perdue account. Industry watchers were both fascinated and tickled by the waves Frank made on Madison Avenue, as dozens of agencies danced attendance around the hard-nosed chicken farmer. One story has it that Frank invited the bigwigs of a prestigious agency to lunch at the Plaza's Oak Room—*they* assumed, so he could deliver the good news that they'd won the account. Nope. They hadn't even survived the first cut. Frank had summoned them to ask for their thoughts about the agencies still in the running. They obliged. By the time Perdue was done, he had pissed off most of the agencies on his list.

SMS—the smallest and youngest of the agencies he approached—was among the five finalists. We, too, had been put through the Perdue wringer. In his *Esquire* article about Frank Perdue, Christian McAdams wrote that Frank called Ed McCabe incessantly, peppering him with questions until

Ed lost his temper. He told Frank he was "a pain in the ass" and that he wasn't sure if the agency still wanted Perdue's account.[28]

We got the account despite, or perhaps because of, the pushback Perdue encountered at SMS. After the tenth meeting with Frank, Marvin jokingly said to him, "You know, Frank, if you spend as much time inspecting your chickens as you have our agency, you have to have the best chickens in the world."

Frank Perdue was hard to please and obsessive about his product. He took nothing at face value. And therein lay the seed for the campaign slogan that would make Frank and his chickens a household name: "It takes a tough man to make a tender chicken." It didn't take our creative gurus, Ed and Sam, long to figure out that Perdue would be the best spokesman (and salesman) for his chickens. Frank was not slick or polished. In fact, he looked a bit like a chicken, with his bald pate, sad eyes, and beak of a nose. And his nasal voice made him sound like one, too. At first, Frank balked at our suggestion that he put himself in front of a camera and *become* the advertising. But the blunt, conversational headlines Ed came up with appealed to Frank. And he got a kick out of skewering the competition.

"Freeze my chickens? I'd sooner eat beef!" And "Everybody's chickens are approved by the government, but only my chickens are approved by me."

"Who cares where the beef is?" said another cheeky headline, accompanied by a photo of Frank holding a drumstick. The full-page ad appeared in the *New York Times* during Wendy's (the fast-food chain) famous "Where's the Beef" campaign.

People loved the ads and they loved Frank. He seemed genuine and reassuring—he refused to say anything in an ad that he himself did not believe. Consumers bought the chickens that they imagined he had personally watched over and nurtured with fresh well water, marigold petals, and food healthier than what most people ate. People decided it was worth it to spend a few cents more per pound to buy a Perdue chicken. And when you're selling millions of chickens a week, that adds up to a lot of money. Frank Perdue became a very wealthy man—certainly the most eccentric one I've ever met. I managed his account for fifteen years and found him to be ornery, driven, intuitive, cheap, and, as Ed had pointed out, a pain in the ass. He had no tolerance for brownnosers. Most of the time, we got along well.

When I showed Frank the media plan for his first television campaign (starring him), he asked how we could be sure that the ads would run at the times listed.

"Frank," I said, "we are running these ads on CBS, NBC, and ABC. They're major corporations. They are reliable. You have to trust that they are going to run what we've contracted for."

Frank squinted at me and said, "Pesky, let me tell you something, and don't ever forget this: I don't trust anyone. I don't even trust Jesus Christ."

Several years later, when we proposed Perdue take advantage of a marketing opportunity that would require an increased advertising expenditure, he called me at home on a Saturday to berate me. I had just sat down for dinner with Wendy and the kids. "Pesky, you guys just want to make more money off of me," he said.

I continued the phone call from the den. "Frank," I said, "you and I have known each other for years. If you haven't realized by now that I have never done anything on your account that wasn't in the best interest of your company, then I can't work with you anymore." By this time, I was yelling, too. "And you know what you can do with your account." I slammed down the phone and stalked into the kitchen. Wendy, Heidi, Lee, and Greg, eyes wide, had stopped eating.

Half an hour later, the phone rang again. It was Frank. He was calling to apologize.

Perdue became a celebrity (which I suspect he enjoyed more than all the money he made), and our advertising was one of the most highly awarded campaigns for several years. If the Volvo account put us on the map, Perdue made our young, independent agency famous. Years later, when we made our pitch for the lucrative Revlon account, founder and CEO Charles Revson told us, "I don't care that you guys have never worked on a cosmetics account; if you can sell chickens like you did for Perdue, you sure as heck can sell my lipsticks." If it hadn't been for Frank

Perdue and his chickens, we may not have caught the eye of Ogilvy & Mather.

Over the years, I've been asked how we were able to make the agency we started on a shoestring such a success. There was no formula, no set strategy. We simply wanted to produce great ads, employ a lot of talented people, and make an indelible imprint on the advertising industry. I don't think any of us expected SMS to take off as quickly as it did.

Consciously or not, we cultivated an environment that felt like a family right from the start. Granted, at times it resembled a rambunctious and somewhat dysfunctional family. "The Manson family," one guy called it.[29] It was creative chaos. There was shouting, and there were insults (most lobbed by Ed, with nearly as many muttered about him behind his back). Sometimes, there was blood. One day, when he was really amped up about an ad he was working on, Ed decided to do push-ups in his office. He fell on his chin. The blood was everywhere.[30]

Scali, McCabe, Sloves could be a grueling place to work. "The home of the 72-hour day," according to some of our employees. Yet it was also a petri dish of creativity. Everything was open for discussion, including ideas that would eventually be tossed out. For many years, our agency was considered *the* place to work in the business because of the cutting-edge creativity of our ads. Which helped us to attract even more creative minds. We welcomed a diversity of talent and encouraged people to learn from one another. In a 1996 commemorative publication, *Scali, McCabe, Sloves: A Look Back*, employees (most of whom I'd worked with) were asked to share thoughts and anecdotes about the firm. Copywriter Tom Nathan wrote, "We unabashedly walked into each other's offices with our vulnerable, newborn ideas and asked opinions from the very same people we were trying to outdo. We respected and helped each other . . . We became better than we thought we could be."[31] Our advertising had to be intelligent, relevant, and humane, and Ed and Sam expected *all* ads to be great. Not just really good. Whether it was a two-square-inch coupon ad or a full-page ad in the *Times*. Earl Carter, one of our senior copywriters, once remarked, "Clients not only got more creative bang for their buck, they got a nuclear blast."[32]

The five of us ran the agency as a team, and the drama and excesses at SMS were somehow smoothed out by the differences in our personalities. Bob Schmetterer, who began his tenure with us as an account executive on the Perdue account and would go on to become the agency's managing director a few years after I left, observed that "The greatness of [SMS], in those days, was the *balance* of partners not the greatness of one . . . No one person or two ran SMS, they all did, they were all responsible for their greatness and the greatness of their advertising and their success."[33]

I don't think Marvin, Ed, Sam, Len, or I gave this dynamic much thought as we were building SMS. We were too busy. Luck had a lot to do with how we came together, and we managed to create something much bigger than any of us could have achieved individually.

By 1987, seven years after we sold the agency and had become part of Ogilvy & Mather, I realized that it was time for me to move on. What I had loved most about "the old" SMS was creating groundbreaking advertising for clients who were like family to us—many of them underdogs in their fields, owners as unconventional as their products. People like Frank Perdue. And Leonard Pines, the patriarch and chairman of Hebrew National. Pines, who was about 5'3", had a large, ebullient presence. After we made our pitch to them, Pines made his way around the long boardroom conference table to congratulate and talk to Ed McCabe. Ed was arguably the best copywriter in the industry at the time—a bit of a rock star. Pines put his hand on Ed's shoulder, looked him in the eye, and said, "I like you! You know why?"

Ed, waiting for the accolade, seemed to grow in stature.

"Because you're short," Pines finished, beaming.

We loved creating great advertising for them all—regardless of the size of the ad or the account (or the owner). For SMS, every ad was the most important ad. Every account, the most important one.

The sale of our agency to Ogilvy & Mather made us wealthy. But there was a trade-off: our agency lost its agility, uniqueness, and creative independence. Our future was now dictated by how many new clients we could bring in every year, how many agencies we could acquire, and how much we could generate in billings. And every year, shareholders would expect more. Excellence was no longer our compass. And that made me increasingly uncomfortable. *More* was rapidly feeling like *less* to me.

Starting the business and putting everything on the line had been easier for me than deciding to leave behind what I had created with my partners. SMS would always be a part of me. But I felt that my part in the agency had run its course.

I retired on January 1, 1988. But I had no intention of slowing down. In my farewell letter to SMS employees, I wrote, "There's an awful lot of world out there, and I've seen only a small part of it." Now I had the freedom to see and do more. I envisioned fresh challenges—adventures on mountains and rivers, epic bike rides, and marathons—and recognition for new accomplishments. I imagined that my life going forward would be rewarding in an entirely different way.

And it would be—eventually. But not in the way I expected. Lee's death and the events that followed changed the way I looked at life, well-being, and fulfillment. It filtered out the fanfare and dissolved my desire for recognition. The son who had so often frustrated me, whose challenges stumped me, and whose essence had somehow eluded me, would, through his death, teach me some of the most important things about life.

"If you don't know how to read, you don't have a life."

These words did not come from a parent or a teacher or a special education professional. They were spoken twenty years ago by a young girl during her first session at Lee Pesky Learning Center with Deb Glaser, our director of education and training.

I was reminded of that young girl's gut-wrenching comment when I received a letter from a woman whose son had been working with our specialists for several months. They had come to LPLC as a last resort. She wrote, "My son can read and spell and write [now], albeit slowly. He can do it. His comprehension is remarkable. At eleven, he already has his choice of colleges picked out . . . But what you should really care about is that my son wants to live."

My son wants to live. As I read on, I learned that a year earlier Peter (not his real name) had made plans to take his own life. He had resolved not to eat, not to drink water, and not to move until he passed away. Peter couldn't understand why he was born with a brain that wouldn't allow him to do what he wanted and needed to do. The help he was able to get at LPLC was not just about overcoming obstacles to learning. It was also about understanding *why* he had struggled. Most important, it represented a new chance at life for this fifth-grader who, for a while, could not see a place for himself in the world.

WHEN LEE PESKY Learning Center had been open for a few weeks and Blossom called to tell me that we had no clients, Lee had only been gone for eighteen months. I was still waking up every morning thinking about him. Missing him. Unwillingly, I was learning to live with a reality that no parent should ever know.

In a way, though, Lee was still there. He was behind every decision I made about the center that now bore his name. Lee was the reason Blossom, Deb, and I were waiting for the phone to ring: so we could help kids like him.

By the end of the first month, we had three clients. It didn't take long for news about Lee Pesky Learning Center to spread—not through advertising, but by word of mouth. Relieved parents telling friends. Teachers hearing from students. Teachers telling other teachers and parents that kids were getting comprehensive and accurate evaluations at LPLC and one-on-one intervention that worked. Soon we had enough clients to add counseling services for children *and* their parents. Children don't learn or grow or thrive in a vacuum. To help the child, we had to be able to help the family, as well.

The stress and frustration associated with learning disabilities can take an enormous toll on everyone around the child, which, in turn, only exacerbates the child's challenges. In her letter to me, Peter's mother shared that their lives had been in shambles before they came to LPLC. "Our entire family needed help," she wrote. We've heard similar stories from parents since we opened our doors. A couple that brought their daughter to LPLC confided that they had been on the verge of divorcing. Once they understood the nature of the challenges their daughter faced, everyone

With my parents, Belle and Lou Pesky, in Long Beach,
New York, 1936.

My brother, Andy, and I, 1942.

With Andy (far left) and our parents at
Wendy's and my wedding, Hampshire
House, New York City, 1961.

On our wedding day.

Andy and I with our
mother.

In 1957 at Fort Dix, New Jersey, I am
Second Lieutenant Pesky, officer in charge
of the infiltration course and later the
hand grenade range, improbably lecturing
100–150 recruits on how not to get blown
up. Good preparation for corporate (and
less lethal) presentations.

Lee and I on Fire Island. In the late '60s, Wendy and the kids spent the summers there, and I would join them on the weekends.

Lee and I in the backyard of our home in Stamford, Connecticut.

Our first big family trip: rafting in the Grand Canyon, 1975. Greg was 7, Lee 10, Heidi 13. Wendy was afraid that Greg would bounce out of the raft into the rapids.

Our weeklong winter camping trip in the Sawtooth Mountains of Idaho, 1978.

Our favorite winter pastime, snowshoeing, was a welcome escape during the 2020 pandemic.

Wendy and I exploring on cross-country skis, 2007.

Looking toward the summit of Kilimanjaro, the highest peak in Africa, on the climb I did for my 50th birthday, 1983.

In 2011, Wendy and I trekked and camped in Torre del Paine, Patagonia. Last stop before Antarctica. Interesting weather!

Climbing Popocatépetl, an active volcano 43 miles south of Mexico City. The 17,800-foot summit can be seen in the distance.

In 1991, I had the opportunity to spend a week traversing the Ruth Glacier at the base of Denali with the editor of *Summit* magazine.

Leander Jones and I, cocaptains of Jamaica High basketball team, with Coach Shannon, 1951.

The start of our 600-mile, 10-day bike trip across the Outback of Australia in 1994. A blistering, solitary, and incredible way to see this remarkable part of the world.

Crossing a flooded road, wondering whether there were crocodiles submerged. An unexpected peril in the dusty Outback.

Always elegant, my princess luxuriating on the ride.

Although we remained at Base Camp, Wendy and
I were invited to participate in the Puja—a Sherpa
ceremony in which climbers pay respect and offer
blessing for safe passage before climbing Mount Everest.

After leaving the Everest Expedition in Tibet, we
traveled by jeep to Nepal. On the Friendship Bridge, we
stood with one foot in Tibet and the other in Nepal.

In 2016, Wendy and I walked 100 miles of the
Camino de Santiago in Spain.

At Heidi's wedding in the Boulder Mountains. Her proud father with her brothers, Greg and Lee.

One of my favorite photos of the five of us, at Heidi's grad school graduation.

Greg, Wendy, Lee, Heidi, Rick, and I. Good thing it's always sunny in Sun Valley. Not sure what we'd have done if it had rained.

Greg and Naomi's wedding in Philadelphia.

The Pesky-Stern ski gang at the top of Baldy in Sun Valley. Michael Stern is Wendy's eldest brother.

The whole family gathered in Barcelona, Spain, in 2011 to celebrate Wendy's and my 50th anniversary.

With our grandchildren, Hope, Talia, Levi, Eliza, and Sam.

Team Lee Pesky Learning Center in 2017 before the start of the NYC Marathon, an annual tradition.

Crossing the finish line of the NYC Marathon with Heidi in 2012, to celebrate my 80th birthday. It was not my fastest time. (Best run ever.)

Running my first New York City Marathon in 1981.

Wendy spotting one of "our" seals on Nantucket—the inspiration for the children's book I wrote and Heidi illustrated, *The Sea and the Seal.*

The partners: Sam Scali, Ed McCabe, Marvin Sloves, Len Hultgren, and I.

Frank Perdue ("the tough man who made tender chickens"), Ed McCabe, and I.

Marching down Fifth Avenue on Solidarity Sunday for Soviet Jewry with Israel Ambassador to the UN Netanyahu, NYC Mayor Koch, and Senator D'Amato, ca. 1984.

Elie Wiesel and I, both speakers at a conference for Soviet Jewry, ca. 1984.

In 1998, LPLC hosted its first Bridges to Learning Conference. From left, Sheldon Horowitz, National Center for Learning Disabilities; Sally Shaywitz, Yale Medical School; Bob Brooks, Harvard Medical School; Bennett Shaywitz, Yale Medical School; Blossom Turk, Executive Director of LPLC; I; and Wendy.

Participating as an executive in residence at Tuck School in 2008. The Lee Pesky Learning Center Case Study was part of the curriculum.

A rare day of reading and relaxation at our cabin in Copper Basin.

The LPLC management team, 2020. From left: Cristianne Lane, Dan Houston, Lindy Crawford, Evelyn Johnson, Laura Moylan, and Matt Scott.

Evelyn Johnson, CEO of Lee Pesky Learning Center.

Blossom Turk, founding executive director, Lee Pesky Learning Center.

With Dr. Patrick Kelly, Lee's neurosurgeon. After Lee passed away, Patrick and I became good friends and started the Brain Tumor Foundation together.

In 2011, I was invited to be the commencement speaker at Boise State University's winter graduation.

Smile, Wit, Love . . . Lee David Pesky, 1972.

in the family was able to find some peace. The parents stopped blaming each other and adjusted their expectations. They stopped being angry with their daughter. They stopped thinking, *You're acting this way because you want to annoy me*—which is all too often how parents misinterpret some of their children's behaviors. Like I did with Lee when I thought he was "acting out." As Anne Clohessy, psychologist and lead evaluator at LPLC, reminds parents, *Behavior is communication*, a sign that something is going on with the child that has not yet been understood.

So many of the obstacles Lee faced weren't *his* problems. They were *my* problems. They were the teachers' and the schools' problems, and the problems of so many others who didn't understand that all minds don't think and learn alike. (And what a boring place the world would be if they did!) Lee faced challenges that only became his problem when we tried to force him to fit into *our* framework of expectations. And into an educational system that wasn't designed for everyone.

Once LPLC had established its credibility helping individual students and their families, widening the circle to include schools was a natural progression. Teachers and schools called to ask for our assistance. How could they better support students with learning disabilities in their classrooms? Could we help them identify students with learning disabilities earlier? Was there anything we could do to help them improve kindergarten through third-grade reading instruction for *all* children? So, we took what we were learning in our work with individual children and created teacher training programs designed to strengthen science-based reading instruction and early detection of learning disabilities. The results were measurably encouraging. When the state legislature learned of our ability to improve reading outcomes in schools, they asked LPLC to draft the early childhood education guidelines for Idaho and passed the Idaho Comprehensive Literacy Act. Eventually, the research we were doing to support our teaching models became an essential part of our mission, and LPLC came to be regarded as a respected authority in the state on evidence-based approaches to learning disabilities and early literacy. Today, LPLC shares its findings and research-based approaches with schools and institutions in multiple states. Even in other countries.

Change happens one child at a time. When we were starting out, it didn't occur to me that we'd be able to help kids beyond those who came through our doors. Lee Pesky Learning Center was my response to the death of our son. In the beginning, it gave me direction and purpose for my grief. It seemed like the best way for our family to remember and honor Lee. Twenty-four years later I am, frankly, blown away by how far we have come. Since its inception, Lee Pesky Learning Center has benefitted more than 100,000 children through its work. One hundred thousand Lees and Peters and others like them.

It has been an unlikely success story. We weren't guided by ambition, five-year plans, or growth targets. It was never my goal for us *to be seen as the best*, nor did we strive to be the biggest. Ego and vanity have no place when you are dealing with the lives of children. Our goal was simply to *do our best* for each child who came through our doors, and, as we grew, to do our best for every child whose life might be improved through our research and teacher training programs.[34]

At the end of the day, 100,000 is just a number—meaningless, unless you see each one of those children as a human being deserving of respect, dignity, and the opportunity to live a fulfilling life. We have a saying at LPLC: *Each child who walks through the door is the most important child.* For us, that begins with the recognition that everyone has a unique learning fingerprint—even people who don't have learning disabilities. No one fingerprint is better or worse than another. They're just different.

Trying to squeeze all students into a one-size-fits-all learning formula would be pointless. So LPLC professionals begin with science-based, well-tested models and then tailor them to the needs of the learner. Fortunately, we don't need to reinvent the wheel for each child. Our methodology draws on a wealth of information, previous successes, and failures. Over time, the information we've gathered on what works and what doesn't has been collated, analyzed, and codified. With every child, that base of knowledge, and how we apply it, is adjusted, expanded, and improved upon.

If a child isn't making progress with us at LPLC or in school, we don't blame the child. We look critically at ourselves. Their lack of progress usually means *we* haven't yet found the right approach for that learner, and our intervention plan needs to be adjusted. This is quite different from what many kids encounter at school or even at home: "failure" is frequently ascribed to laziness, lack of discipline, immaturity, insufficient motivation or concentration, a bad attitude—you name it. So often, when we blame the child, we're missing the point. We're seeing our expectations, not the child. We're seeing what we think are their failures, when, most often, they're ours.

There is infinitely more to a person than what they struggle with. Kids should never be defined by their learning differences, and I love it when they feel empowered to point this out to adults. Like Jacob, for example—a sixth-grader who has dyslexia and dysgraphia. He offered to share his story at Storyfort, a venue for authors, artists, poets, and other storytellers at Boise's annual Treefort Music Fest. Unfortunately, the 2020 festival had to be postponed due to the pandemic, but Jacob and his mother, Lisa, agreed to be interviewed on Idaho's NPR station, Boise State Public Radio.[35]

During the interview, Jacob politely corrected the host of the radio show, Gemma Gaudette. "One thing I heard you say is that dyslexia is a disability for me," he said. "It *kind* of is—with reading. But at the same time, it's really not, because it gets me advanced in other areas—like creativity." Jacob likes to perform. In fact, he volunteered to go on stage and tell others about his experience with learning disabilities. Jacob was so excited about his presentation and determined to do a good job that he prepared his speech months in advance. "I'm pretty used to performing," the sixth-grader assured Gemma when she expressed amazement at his courage. "I like being in front of people. At the same time, it makes me nervous. And afterward, I'm happy about it."

Jacob sees another advantage in his experience with dyslexia. "Possibly, eventually, it's going to get me into a higher spot when I get to high school and college. I'm going to have to work harder than people who don't usually work that hard." Jacob, like so many other kids with learning disabilities, is used to working hard. He views his progress in overcoming challenges as a strength. And progress is possible because Jacob *understands* his challenges, as do the people around him.

So much of what his mother, Lisa, shared with the interviewer also resonated with me. First was Lisa's recognition that her anxiety for Jacob was adding to his learning challenges; stress begets more stress, and stress impedes learning. But the part that got me choked up was his mother's realization that she needed to let her son *be who he was*. Although Jacob was becoming a stronger reader thanks to the strategies he was learning at LPLC, reading would probably always be stressful for him. But, Lisa said, "He does other stuff that he's super excited about." Lisa came to the realization that she needed to see her son's reading within a larger context of achievement and progress.

What a beautiful insight. Sometimes, the box in which we put our children is too small for them. I had a box I wanted all three of my children to fit into. A box built of my experiences, my ambitions, my interests. Also my insecurities. My box had tennis and opera, not dirt bikes and the Grateful Dead. Excellence at school and in sports featured prominently in my box. It was not a good fit for Lee. I know this now. Maybe it wasn't ideal for Heidi or Greg, either.

ADVERTISING HAS LITTLE if anything to do with helping children overcome obstacles to learning. Yet, I believe that each layer of one's life quietly prepares one for the next—often in unexpected ways. Much of what I learned and experienced at Scali, McCabe, Sloves enabled me to do what I did with Lee Pesky Learning Center. The first connection was a financial one: SMS gave me the means to launch and sustain a nonprofit organization in the name of a child I lost. But the two experiences are connected in other, more important ways—by the richness of collaboration and a familial culture, the unswerving dedication to a worthy mission, and attracting great people through integrity and excellence.

Like SMS, Lee Pesky Learning Center had the opportunity to "go big" by becoming part of a larger institution—Boise State University. An arrangement of that kind would have afforded LPLC many advantages: financial security, access to resources, and enhanced visibility and prestige. The future of LPLC would have been secure. But we chose not to do it. While we continue to work closely with Boise State's College of Education in ways that continually enhance our ability to help children, we didn't want our core values to become diluted. Our scientific and creative agility would have been subsumed by the university's more rigid structure and bureaucracy. LPLC would have become guided by Boise State's vision instead of our own.

I've also been asked by enthusiastic and long-standing supporters why we've chosen not to open offices in other cities. Why not take Lee Pesky Learning Center's approach and duplicate it elsewhere? The simple answer is bigger would not equate to better in our case. We've found that we can expand the range of our impact in more effective ways. We do so through strategic partnerships with universities, researchers, and foundations. And by continuing to train teachers who can reach far more children than we can. Teachers are at the frontlines of learning and can provide science-based reading instruction to *all* children in their classrooms, and they can spot those who may be struggling with learning differences. We will continue to share our findings and methodologies with as many institutions and schools around the world as we can. This is how we can do our best for as many children as possible. Remaining independent and true to our original purpose has been the right decision.

WHEN I WAS making my mark in advertising, I associated success with personal achievements, public recognition, and wealth. I never gave much thought to humility. Today, I couldn't be prouder that LPLC's mission is *not* about me or any one person who works there. Our achievement is measured by what we accomplish for others: making a sustainable difference in the lives of kids and their families. Our impact does not come from wanting to *be the best*, but by making a commitment to *do one's best*, every day.

Humility lies at the foundation of our quest for excellence. Our CEO, Evelyn Johnson, thinks of LPLC as a "learning institution." Not because we are in the business of helping people learn. But because we—those who work at, or on behalf of, LPLC—always have more to learn.

From whom do we learn the most? From the children we are teaching. Every child who comes to us for help gives us the opportunity to gain a deeper understanding of how the brain works and how people learn differently. Research-driven teaching is a cumulative experience that is enriched by each person we get to know and work with and help—which, in turn, makes us better prepared to help the next child, and the next.

At Lee Pesky Learning Center, each child is our most important teacher.

Just as Lee was mine.

Chapter 11

Together

When we started Lee Pesky Learning Center, we focused primarily on learning disabilities—neurological processing issues that can present lifelong challenges. In twenty-four years, our mission hasn't changed, but the lens through which we view our work has widened. In LPLC's 2020 annual impact report, "Overcoming Obstacles to Learning," the term *learning disabilities* is mentioned only once. While learning differences still lie at the heart of the expertise LPLC brings to all its endeavors, we have come to view such challenges in a broader context. They can be the result of learning disabilities, but they can also be the result of structural poverty and structural racism, which can impede one's access to quality education. Whatever the cause, we need to work together to address obstacles to learning. Literacy affects everyone.

"I'M NOT A superfast reader now," Israel said, "but I'm a successful reader."

The 32-year-old who sat across from me in an Italian restaurant in Boise had an open and engaging demeanor. He had ridden his bike the eight miles from his home to meet me for dinner—and his final interview for the position of codirector of LPLC. Israel Catz's credentials were impressive: he was a graduate of Middlebury College and had a Master's from Harvard Graduate School of Education. He'd worked as a teacher in Boise and served as a Peace Corps volunteer in Madagascar, where he also founded a nonprofit to combat hunger and illiteracy. Yet one of the most striking things about Israel didn't appear on his résumé: he did not attend school until he was fifteen.

Israel was born in a place called Robie Creek, a collection of cabins and trailers along the edge of the Boise National Forest, with its two million acres of mountains, spruce forests, rivers, and lakes. The recreational possibilities are endless, but services in Robie Creek are limited. There is no cell service. No gas station or grocery store. And school is 38 miles away.

Robie Creek is not unusual. There are dozens of beautiful rural communities in Idaho, many of them underserved, some literally "off the map." Tara Westover describes such a place, her hometown in southeastern Idaho, in *Educated*—a stark account of her struggle to educate herself. Like Westover, Israel's early exposure to formal education was limited. Raised in a trailer home, he and his siblings were homeschooled.

"There is no standard, no prescribed curriculum for homeschooling in Idaho. There is nothing," Israel explained. He could barely read. He thinks of it as a kind of "environmental dyslexia" (not a technical term, but a way of describing his former inability to read), which I found interesting.

When he was fourteen, Israel was doing odd jobs to help his family make ends meet: construction, painting houses, you name it. A chance encounter led to an unexpected opportunity to attend an independent school in Boise on a needs-based scholarship. When Israel arrived at Riverstone International School, he could read about fifteen words a minute. The average eighth-grade student reads at a rate of 200–250 words per minute.

"There was a huge learning curve for me. I was not a skilled student at that time," Israel told me. Initially, his goal was to attend school long enough to get his GED (Graduate Equivalency Degree). But he didn't stop there.

Israel was offered the position at Lee Pesky Learning Center, and although he wasn't with us long, we benefited from his contributions and perspective. As I write this, Israel is working on his doctorate at Harvard—a trajectory that seems remarkable to me given where he began. But this is not a "pull-yourself-up-by-the-bootstraps" story. As Israel tells it, the remarkable part of his story is not what he accomplished, but the role that luck played in his life: he was given the chance to go to a school where people believed in and supported him—an educational experience that enabled him, with hard work, to overcome obstacles and pursue a path that would have been improbable otherwise. "One of my goals," Israel said, "is never to forget that luck played a role in my outcome. In my privilege."

Israel has four siblings, but he is the only person in his family to have graduated high school. "For me, education has been like a magic wand or a superpower, bringing benefits I could not have possibly imagined," Israel said. "It has literally opened the world to me. The most important gift is learning that something you once deeply held to be true was wrong. As a result, you learn to question everything—a healthy and powerful notion that allows you to live a fuller life." Education is the foundation on which layers of experiences are built. For Israel, the layers have included teaching, travel, languages, nonprofit work, new skills, grad school, and giving back: "People trust you based on how you carry yourself, what you know, and the work you've done. And because of that, you get to impact other people's lives, help educate others, and improve systems for the betterment of people. And all that comes through education."

Most troubling for him is that he considers himself the least intelligent of his siblings. Israel has chosen to be an educator so that he can help to make "uncommon outcomes" like his common. He believes, as do I, that it shouldn't be a matter of luck or circumstance for children to have access to schools and educators prepared to meet their needs—whether you are a kid in rural Idaho who cannot read, a kid in Chicago who is traumatized by racism, or a kid in San Antonio whose first language is not English.

"We have to do this better," Israel says, "because there's a lot of potential being lost."

When I was growing up, it didn't occur to me that there might be an *if* about school. My brother and I had access to good public schools, and our parents supported us in our pursuit of learning. I was not a stellar student academically, but I got the tools I needed to navigate through life. School was a place for me to figure out what I was good at (athletics, doing math in my head, being a leader) and what was hard for me (studying, taking tests). My high school in Queens exposed me to a diversity of people and ways of thinking—a community that cultivated my curiosity and a desire to try new things. School expanded the options available to me and helped me find a fulfilling path. Education made my life better.

When Wendy and I were raising our kids, we saw education as the means for them to *maximize* achievement. To "up their game." Attending the "best" college they could get into was important to us and to them, but it was not a matter of survival. It was the icing on the cake. Lee was unlucky to have been born with learning disabilities when there was minimal help for kids who had them. But we had the contacts and resources to ensure that he got support in other ways, like a choice of schools and the assistance of tutors. All three of our children benefited from advantages and connections that come with privilege. And Lee, who struggled most, got what many children with learning challenges don't get: second chances. When his primary school told us that Lee didn't "fit in," we pushed back. When Lee's freshman year grades didn't qualify him to return to Lafayette College for sophomore year, I asked to meet with the dean. Wendy and I were in a position to mitigate at least some of the challenges Lee experienced and to give him a leg up when he needed it.

When I was a kid, I didn't think of myself as privileged. But I realize now that I was. And my progress in life has also involved the luck of being in the right place at the right time and meeting people who helped me along the way. In his commencement speech at Princeton in 2012, author Michael Lewis told the graduates, "Above all, recognize that if you have had success, you have also had luck—and with luck comes obligation. You owe a debt, and not just to your Gods. You owe a debt to the unlucky."[36] For me, this manifests in a sense of personal obligation and a desire to offer a helping hand, particularly to those who have been left out or left behind. It's the right thing to do. And I believe that I'm better off as an individual when we're all doing well.

For many years, our motto at Lee Pesky Learning Center was "Every child's triumph in learning is a victory for our world." When a child's potential goes unfulfilled, it's not only a personal tragedy. It diminishes us as a community.

WE ARE BY several measures the richest country in the world, and we do a lousy job taking care of our children. I was pleased to see that this was the subject of the 2019 year-end alumni newsletter I received from the Tuck Center for Business, Government & Society. Everyone ought to be paying attention to the facts the editors highlighted.[37] Notably, they point to *The Nation's Report Card*, issued by the US Department of Education: Sixty percent of American fourth-graders and eighth-graders are not proficient in reading.[38] Think about that for a moment. *More than half of our kids cannot read at grade level.*

This should shock us, but it doesn't. National reading scores haven't budged in 30 years.[39] Kids in the U.S get an education roughly on par with their peers in Mongolia and Uzbekistan. I came across this jarring comparison in a *New York Times* column by Nicholas Kristof.[40] According to the Social Project Index, which looks at 163 countries based on 50 metrics of well-being, the United States ranks 91st in access to quality education.[41] Their analysis is not an outlier. UNICEF's Innocenti Report Card assesses the well-being of children in 29 of the world's advanced economies. In 2013, the U.S. was 27th in education—higher only than Greece and Romania.[42] These are just some of the many indicators pointing to the dismal state of learning in our country.

Poverty and the systemic inequities that contribute to it have a lot to do with our nation's literacy challenges. Twelve million children in this country live in poverty—one in five. It's no surprise that poverty limits access to quality education. Schools in less affluent communities tend to be underresourced, which affects everything from the teacher-student ratio to the breadth of classes and programs offered (including music, languages, and the arts) and the quality of facilities like gyms, computer labs, and playgrounds. Consider, also, the financial investment some of us make (myself included) to give our kids "an edge" in the increasingly competitive educational landscape: extracurricular activities, study abroad programs, tutors, the latest technologies, college entrance consultants, and

SAT prep courses, to name just a few of the extras now deemed "essential." Meanwhile, far too many parents are worried about whether they'll be able to make next month's rent.

And therein lies another, more insidious, relationship between poverty and literacy: Deprivation erodes a child's physical and emotional abilities to learn. Stress factors such as poor nutrition, housing insecurity, and limited exposure to a language-rich environment impede neuroprocessing and long-term brain development, resulting in something like an acquired learning disability. If approximately one in five people are *born* with some form of learning disability, how many more people are we burdening with such challenges after they are born? We have only to look at incarceration statistics to gain some insight: it's estimated that three out of five people in American prisons can't read.[43] Literacy challenges and poverty reinforce each other in a malignant cycle to the detriment of us all.

Through a combination of neglect and design, we've ended up with a system with built-in obstacles for a large swath of children. Because of structural inequalities and systemic barriers, the likelihood of getting a good education from an early age has too much to do with the luck of the draw, like who your parents are, the color of your skin, or where you live. As someone who benefited immeasurably from public education, I am baffled and, frankly, ashamed to see how our society is failing its children. It saddens and infuriates me when I hear people speak of the most vulnerable kids as "other people's children." As if it had nothing to do with them. Yet *everyone's children* will be the workers, managers, innovators, and business owners who drive our future economy. They will be our teachers and health-care providers. They will be our neighbors. The citizens who participate in our democracy. If we wanted to engineer a chain with weak links, we couldn't be doing a better job.

The challenges facing education in our country are complicated and overwhelming, and I don't pretend to have the answers. Perhaps there is no one, grand solution. Or, we lack the collective will to find it. A longtime LPLC supporter once remarked, "Alan, you guys are like David trying to take on Goliath. Is there really any chance you're going to be able to make any significant systemic changes?"

My answer to him: "We will do it step by step. Every day, we will do *something*."

THE HUMAN BRAIN, with its billions of neurons, synapses, and glial cells, is marvelously pliable. Throughout our lives we continue to learn new skills, and we find new ways to do old things. When it comes to learning language skills, however, the biggest gains are made at a young age. Neuroscience tells us that the ideal time to get kids started in reading and writing is between the ages of three and five. Remediation when kids are older (even when they become adults) is possible and should be actively supported. But it needs to be far more intensive and time-consuming at that stage than what it takes to get young children off on the right foot to begin with.

This is one of the most compelling reasons behind the push for universal pre-K education. Unfortunately, we're all over the map on this as a country. Most states offer some form of voluntary pre-K, but not every child is enrolled.[44] A handful of states, including Idaho, don't mandate kindergarten attendance. In fact, Idaho's compulsory school attendance only begins at age 7. *At a minimum*, early childhood education and kindergarten should be made available to all children. And ideally, all classrooms would provide science-based reading instruction—that is, an instructional approach based on the extensive body of research about the cognitive processes involved in learning to read. This methodology, also known as evidence-based instruction, relies on practices that have been proven to work. Where this approach is used, more students are likely to be reading at grade level by the time they enter first grade.

If you're like me, you probably learned to read by first looking at colorful picture books with simple words. You expanded your vocabulary as you progressed, practiced spelling and writing, and worked on reading comprehension and reading fluency. These are all important components of reading. I learned to read quite easily, so it never occurred to me that this approach wasn't adequate for some of my peers—that they might have problems relating the sounds they heard to the letters they saw on the page. The letter pattern *-tion*, for example, is found at the end of many words. It sounds like *shun*, but that's not how it's written. When kids are taught this pattern, it can help them decode words they haven't seen before, like *caution* or *nation* or *relation*.[45] Decoding these letter-sound relationships is what is known as phonics. And the fact is, many kids struggle with reading if they haven't had the benefit of explicit phonics instruction.

Extensive research has shown that the most effective reading instruction for *all* learners includes phonics instruction (decoding)—a key element of a science-based approach. According to literacy expert Louisa Moats, who has consulted with LPLC since its early days, reading is nothing less than rocket science. In her acclaimed resource for teachers, *Reading IS Rocket Science*, Dr. Moats makes the case that the difficulty of teaching reading in our schools has been seriously underestimated.

Unfortunately, too many of our teachers (through no fault of their own) have not received strong training in the science of reading. And many who have had the training end up working in school systems that are not supportive of evidence-based practices. Or they're not held accountable to use those practices. Other teachers are just missing the support needed to solidify their skills. As a result, too many children fail to become strong readers—even if they don't have learning disabilities—which contributes to the literacy gaps I described earlier. That's why Lee Pesky Learning Center's team chose to use the expertise we've developed helping kids with learning disabilities to support teachers to use evidence-based reading instruction in their classrooms. High-quality, early learning experiences for as many children as possible is the key to closing the literacy gap in our country.

LPLC advocates science-based reading instruction because it's a tool that we know works. At its core, LPLC's early literacy work is a matter of inclusion. When we're able to have more teachers using science-based instruction, we have a better chance of lifting up *all* children. The Idaho Early Literacy Project (IELP) led by LPLC is one such endeavor. A project based on the science of reading, it also shows what can be accomplished when we come together and focus on what is possible, on what we can do better.

Launched by Lee Pesky Learning Center in 2018, IELP is unusual for a number of reasons. First, it involves seven school districts that serve some of the state's most vulnerable populations, reaching more than 200 educators and over 3,000 students (pre-K–2nd grade). Second, as a multi-year initiative, a team of six reading coaches has the opportunity to work with the same schools for three years to build and solidify best practices in reading instruction. Third, and perhaps most important, the project enjoys a broad base of support: Idaho's State Department of Education, teachers and administrators, hundreds of individual donors, and one of the largest private foundations in the country. As I write this, the project is two-thirds completed, and, notwithstanding the obstacles posed by the 2020 pandemic, the improvement in reading outcomes has been remarkable. After the first year alone, the number of kindergarten students reading at or above grade level increased from 32 percent to 57 percent.[46] In other words, only about one-third of the students were reading at grade level when the program began in the fall, and nearly twice as many were by the end of the school year.[47]

The effectiveness of the project has a lot to do with *how* the science is delivered and shared. And that comes down to the people involved. I would like to tell you about a few of them.

Dr. Evelyn Johnson, LPLC's CEO, is the driving force behind IELP, and her contributions to the methodology that undergirds the project cannot be overstated. "My role in this project," Evelyn explained, "was to support the team and guide their work, ensuring that we developed evidence-based approaches to coaching, that we did the hard work of observing teachers and giving them feedback on their reading instruction, and that we collected data on student outcomes so that we would know if we had been successful in our goal to help students in Idaho learn to read better."

A bit of background about Evelyn: she is a disciplined and innovative researcher in the field of special education and a gifted teacher. Her desire to help children binds all these qualities. School was Evelyn's saving grace when she was a child. At the age of eight, she knew she wanted to be a teacher. Now her work advances the nation's understanding of learning and benefits more people than she could have imagined. A long-distance runner, Evelyn leads LPLC's New York City Marathon team every year—our most strenuous fund-raising effort. (Our first team marathon shirt, in 2013, was emblazoned with the words *Learning is not a sprint. It's a marathon*.) She recruits board members, supporters, friends, and Pesky family members to join her in the run. Evelyn's commitment and enthusiasm are unflagging, and this spirit shines through in her work.

It's hard to say no to Evelyn. Richard Osguthorpe, the former dean of Boise State University's College of Education, observed that his university colleagues not only didn't say no to the initiatives Evelyn proposed, *they actively wanted to be part of them*. Whenever a proposal came from LPLC and Evelyn, he said, everyone knew it was for a greater good and that there was no hidden agenda or ulterior motive. "And doesn't everyone want to be part of something that's for the greater good?" he asked.

Boise State University and LPLC have had a thriving partnership, the Special Education Collaborative, for many years. Collaboration in the field of education is not unusual, but this partnership is. From Richard's perspective, it's a collaboration in the truest sense of the word. The benefits to Boise State's College of Education were exponential: after joining forces with LPLC on certain projects and grant proposals, their investment in research skyrocketed, they could provide world-class pedagogical opportunities for their students through internships at LPLC, and the College's national rankings shot up. Richard jokes that when he first took over as dean, before the Special Education Collaborative had gained momentum, he had problems just getting local newspapers to return his calls. A few years later, however, National Public Radio was calling him out of the blue, wanting to talk about the College of Education. "I started telling them about the Special Education Collaborative, and they said, 'Hey! That's the story we want to do. We want to do a story on Lee Pesky Learning Center.'" And they did. The Boise State-LPLC partnership was featured on NPR's *Weekend Edition with Scott Simon*.[48]

The "we're-all-in-this-together" ethos of LPLC, Richard says, has had positive ripples throughout the state. The staff at LPLC take the time to build relationships in the educational community and in state government, and they are eager to share their experience and expertise. In doing so, LPLC has engendered trust and enhanced the credibility of the teaching profession in Idaho. It's an approach that has paved the way for large-scale collaborative efforts like the Idaho Early Literacy Project. Evelyn and her colleagues know how challenging teaching can be. Rather than blaming teachers for failure (too often the default mode), LPLC offers a model that can help improve educational outcomes by working in concert with teachers and public schools.

"The schools respect that," Richard said. "[LPLC has] created a great environment for improving education without trying to tear anybody else down."

Cristianne Lane exemplifies this spirit. She heads the Early Literacy Project for LPLC and has worked with teachers across the state for years. Cristianne joined LPLC in 2008 as our Professional Development Director. She *loves* her job. Cristianne radiates excitement about learning, and there is always a smile in her voice.

Here's a typical day for Cristianne on the Literacy Project: She catches an early morning flight to Spokane, WA, rents a car, and drives an hour and a half across the border, back into Idaho, to Priest River. She arrives at one of the elementary schools in the district just before classes begin. The teachers know Cristianne well because she comes every month to spend time with them in their classrooms and to be available before and after school for questions. The teachers have already participated in her day-long kick-off training, and they are working with the literacy prac-tices and materials she has provided. Cristianne and her colleagues collect ideas from the teachers in all of the participating districts on what they find works best in their classrooms based on what was presented in the training, and she shares the ideas with everyone, acting as an information hub of sorts on best practices for all educators in the program. When she's back in Boise they hear from her regularly via email. LPLC is a helpline and resource available to the teachers during the school year as questions and challenges arise: "How do I handle this particular situation with this student?" Or, "I have a child who's not responding as well as others with this approach—what do you suggest?"

Teachers trust Cristianne and her team of coaches because they are consistent, and they follow up. Their only purpose is to support teachers in their efforts to measurably improve their students' ability to read.

"I won't kid you, though," Cristianne said. "Not all teachers are thrilled when an outsider first comes into their classroom. I've walked in their shoes, and I know how difficult it is. I also don't know a teacher out there who is not dedicated and who does not want what's best for children. So, when we come into a teacher's classroom—their domain— the last thing we want to do is come across as the know-it-all of reading instruction. We are there to work *with* them, not to tell them what they've been doing wrong." LPLC professional development coaches do a lot of observing and listening in the beginning. Everyone on Cristianne's team has had extensive classroom teaching experience.

When I asked what her secret is, to my delight Cristianne used a sports analogy (even though, she admits, she doesn't watch or play sports). "Working with teachers on best practices in reading instruction is like coaching a team," she said. "First of all, you have to be there to observe them play. Second, you're not just coaching a team—you're also coaching individual athletes who each have different strengths and styles, and who all want the team to win.

"But not everyone is going to get there the same way," Cristianne added. "We need to be respectful of where each teacher is in her or his professional development." This means figuring out what a teacher needs in order to implement best practices in her classroom. When Cristianne suggests an adjustment in a teacher's approach, it is not necessarily a matter of poor instruction on the teacher's part—rather, that the instruction just needs to be more intentional or targeted to specific literacy skills.

What do teachers think of the relationship-building approach Cristianne and her team use? Susie Luckey, principal of Idaho Hills Elementary School, said, "Cristianne gives us information that is research-based and will make a difference for our kids. It's not sugar-coated. You know they're not selling a product."

In other words, their work is not *transactional*. LPLC works to serve teachers and their needs, and that requires relationships. No matter how solid the science is, or how effective the approaches to reading instruction are, if LPLC coaching were delivered in a lecturing or dogmatic manner it wouldn't work. Coaching must take place in the context of an established relationship and in the spirit of partnership.

Educators like Susie Luckey are an essential part of this story, too. I am in awe of what she and her colleagues are doing in their school district (West Bonner County). In the first year of IELP, their schools achieved the greatest improvements in the state—and under very challenging circumstances. Susie gives much of the credit to LPLC for the support the district received from Cristianne. But it goes deeper than that: Susie and her colleagues were actively focused on moving the needle on literacy well before IELP began in 2018.

Priest River lies at the confluence of the Priest and Pend Oreille rivers in the Idaho Panhandle. It's a thirty-minute drive to Canada and a seven-hour drive to Boise on roads winding through heavily timbered mountains. For Susie, the area her family has called home for 130 years is "God's Country." It's beautiful all year round.

Susie is a fourth-generation member of a family that came to Priest River from Italy in the late 1800s along with hundreds of other Italian immigrants to help build the Great Northern Railroad. Timber, mining, and fur trading attracted hardy people from all over the world to this beautiful area that was first home to the indigenous Kallispel people. The names of the rivers, lakes, mountains, and towns reflect this mingling of cultures.

Priest River's fortunes have been closely tied to the timber industry. At one time, it was one of the fastest-growing cities in northern Idaho. Today, the economy is not strong. Some logging and farming jobs remain, but many residents now commute to Spokane for higher-paying jobs. Others have carved out occupations in tourism and outdoor recreation.

As in other areas of Idaho, many children in Susie's district start school a couple of years behind in their reading skills. There may be many reasons for this—such as school resources stretched thin, the logistical challenge of getting kids to school in a rural area, skepticism about the benefits of early childhood education, and even the allocation of resources between sports and academics. "Oftentimes, athletics seem to be more prized than education," Susie observed. But she doesn't mean it as a slight. "If we could get as many people excited about academics as we can about football and basketball games, that would be awesome." She and her fellow educators have not been sitting around waiting for that to happen, because they've witnessed how kids light up when they make a breakthrough in reading.

The evidence-based reading practices Susie and others first learned from LPLC trainers sixteen years earlier were an eye-opener for educators in the district. "Our belief [in science-based reading] changed because of what we were seeing," Susie said. "Our data were showing us that our kids were reading like they'd never read before. And we certainly didn't want to stop doing what was working."

Susie and her colleagues knew they wouldn't be able to make sustainable improvements in literacy unless they worked together. Everyone needed to be on the same page. This was not a competition to see which teacher could get the best results. Rather, it was a collaboration designed to help all teachers get the best possible outcomes for their students.

The district educators began by creating a literacy cadre. That word choice, *cadre*, tells you a lot: these teachers meant business. The literacy cadre gives them a structure and forum to discuss and share effective reading instruction practices. They didn't stop there. Many of the children in the community, they realized, don't have books in their homes because their families can't afford them. So the teachers, in partnership with the Priest River Community Foundation, placed bookshelves around town—at the food bank, at the laundromat, at the Les Schwab Tire Center—and filled them with free children's books so kids could grab them whenever they were out and about with their parents.

Several years ago, the district also chose to take on a Professional Learning Community (PLC) model. PLCs first came into use by schools in the 1990s, designed to foster grade-level collaborations among teachers for the purpose of continued learning and greater consistency of teaching practices. According to All Things PLC, "professional learning communities operate under the assumption that the key to improved learning for students is continuous job-embedded learning for educators."[49] PLCs can vary quite a bit in scope, implementation, and effectiveness, depending on the school.

For the educators of West Bonner County, the PLC framework has been immensely helpful. "When you take on that model," Susie explained, "you're always asking yourselves and each other, 'What do we want the kids to learn? How are we going to get there? What do we do when they're not learning?'" And although not all teachers come from the same viewpoint on everything, having collaborative structures in place gives them the tools to work through differences of opinion. Susie's emphasis always seems to be on "we." I'm not surprised that she was honored as the Idaho National Distinguished Principal in 2018.

Overall, the three elementary schools of the West Bonner school district saw a 60 percent improvement in reading levels in the first year of their participation in the Literacy Project. By the time the district applied to participate in IELP, the educators of Priest River and the surrounding communities had already cemented a shared vision that required improvements in literacy instruction. The teachers already knew how to work and learn together with that important goal in mind. They continue to do it because they care, and because it matters.

In a school district the size of West Bonner, getting 225 young readers up to grade-level reading before they enter 3rd grade is a big deal. These children will have the skills they need to move ahead in their academics. They'll have a better chance of graduating from high school in an area where dropout rates tend to be high. (I'm told that some theorists now use the term "pushout" instead of "dropout.") And children who become confident readers will become literate adults who have more options and choices available to them. They will be more empowered to strengthen their communities.

Susie, Cristianne, and Evelyn are just a few of the extraordinary people forging solutions and a better way forward for children every day. They measure their achievement by the improvement in the young lives entrusted to their care. They love what they do, and they pursue it with determination and passion. To my mind, this is sacred work: shepherding other people's children—our children—as they learn and prepare themselves for the rest of their lives.

Teaching is hard. It's an applied science, so understanding how the science of learning works, how reading should be taught, is only half of the equation. Delivering it in a way that is engaging, consistent, responsive, and thoughtful is important, too. There is a lot of nuance in teaching because every student is different. No one learns in quite the same way. We have high expectations of our children's teachers, and from what I can see, we don't give them nearly the support they need or the recognition they deserve.

THE KELLOGG FOUNDATION chose to underwrite the Idaho Early Literacy Project because Lee Pesky Learning Center's approach is getting results. Moreover, they believe the methodology can be replicated elsewhere and that it translates well across a variety of settings—whether a Head Start preschool or a district second-grade class. Because of the success of IELP, the Kellogg Foundation has decided to expand its partnership with LPLC with a new directive: developing a professional development model for caregivers to children, from birth to age five. After testing the model in Idaho, LPLC hopes to expand the program nationally.

Supporting young learners contributes to the well-being of our country, and many private foundations, businesses, and state legislatures see investment in early learning as a workforce capacity issue. Business schools often speak of the importance of investing in "human capital." There's no question that an educated and capable workforce is essential to the long-term vibrancy of our economy. But the importance of education in our society goes beyond dollars and cents. The ability to earn a living is a matter of individual well-being and dignity. The father in me cringes when I hear the term "human capital." It feels dehumanizing to speak of human beings in the same way one might speak of manufacturing plants and equipment. I think back to Lee and the reason why we started Lee Pesky Learning Center. And I think of Heidi and Greg and their children. Of other people's children. Every human being deserves a decent first chance—not an accidental second chance—at a life they find fulfilling. And education lies at the heart of that potential.

I BELIEVE MOMENTUM and magnetism are generated when individuals come together for a greater good. The Lee Pesky Learning Center is where it is today because we have not forged ahead on our own. We've always invited others to join us in our mission. The LPLC specialists, coaches, and researchers have learned to balance the rigor of science with an ethos of compassion, humility, and inclusion. Inherent in everything they do—be it diagnostic evaluations, one-on-one remediation sessions, counseling for families, or professional development for teachers to advance early literacy—is the desire to understand, connect, and build trust.

Working together always *sounds* wonderful. But in practice, it can be painstaking and uncomfortable. When Susie Luckey speaks of her collaborative work with fellow educators, for example, she's very open about the fact there are (and will always be) differences of opinion among teachers. But agreeing on everything is not the objective of their literacy cadre. What they *do* agree on is that all their students should be able to read and that an evidence-based approach to teaching reading works. They have made a commitment to cooperative frameworks—the cadre, the Idaho Early Literacy Project, a Professional Learning Community model—that will help them achieve their goal while providing a safe place to work through their differences to better teach and support all children.

For me, this is also the essence of Lee Pesky Learning Center. The advancements we've made in learning are a testimony to the magnifier effect of collaboration and evidence-based solutions that are offered with respect and empathy. In a world that feels increasingly fractured and partisan, Lee Pesky Learning Center offers an example of how we can find common ground by creating a space where learning never ends.

Chapter 12

Perspective

Our eyes were fixed on the eighteen-inch screen of our first color TV. Heidi and Lee were next to us on the couch in our den. Greg, only 11 months old, sat on Wendy's lap. It was July 20, 1969. With millions of others, we watched transfixed as Apollo 11 touched down, and a human being stepped onto the surface of the moon for the first time. For such a triumphant moment, the Apollo 11 moon landing was oddly peaceful. A welcome respite from the wars, assassinations, and racist atrocities of the 1960s. Neil Armstrong, Michael Collins, and Buzz Aldrin were *on the moon*. They were in their thirties when they landed on the moon—only three years older than I was at the time. I wondered what it had taken for them to get to that moment, what they had to sacrifice.

When the 50th anniversary of the first moon landing came around in 2019, I was immersed in work on this book and juggling my usual myriad interests and projects. Apollo 11 retrospectives and images popped up everywhere online, the subject of cable talk shows and conversations on NPR. Few captured the momentousness and singularity of the event. I stared at the photos and found myself thinking of the moon landing from a different perspective—this time, considering the Earth through the eyes of Armstrong, Collins, and Aldrin. How did *they* feel and what were *they* thinking as they gazed up from their landing place on the moon in the Sea of Tranquility? Their view of our planet, as seen by the photos they took, is astonishingly beautiful. The Earth, a perfect orb suspended in a sea of black. Shapes of blue, green, and gold, partially obscured by swirls of white and gray. In the photos, you can make out the landmasses of continents, but no lines claiming territory or country. No human-made barriers or divisions. Just a beautiful planet shared by three and a half billion people, many of them looking at the moon when the photos were taken, while three men, 234,000 miles away, looked up toward the Earth. Perhaps, I thought, the moon landing was not so much a story of heroic achievement as it was a remarkable story about us all. So many people looking up, bound together in a singular moment of wonder.

THE PEOPLE WHO have had the greatest influence on my life are those who challenged me the most and broadened my perspective. Some I didn't know, like Bobby Kennedy and Lou Gehrig, inspired me with their words and deeds. Lee forced me to take an uncomfortable look at myself and the lens through which I viewed our relationship. My father's mentoring was silent, so understated that it took me decades to recognize and appreciate the gifts he gave me. Wendy has shown me how strong one can be in a quiet, modest way, reminding me periodically, "Not everyone thinks like you, Alan." And why should they?

Bayless Manning took that wisdom a step further. A friend and mentor, Bayless counseled me to "think with the other person's head." I don't always succeed in real time, but when I take the time to put considered thought into my words—when I write a letter or prepare a speech—I am always guided by his advice. We were introduced at a reception for the former governor of Idaho, Cecil Andrus. "Alan, here's someone you should meet," the governor said. "Two former New Yorkers in Idaho—I think you two might have something in common."

We did, although Bayless was way out of my league—a wunderkind often described by his peers as a visionary and a Renaissance man. Top of his class at Yale (twice—undergrad and law school), a member of the team that broke the Japanese code in WWII, dean of Stanford Law School, the first president of the Council on Foreign Relations, Bayless was also conversant in French, German, Norwegian, Japanese, Spanish, and Latin.[50] This was a man who knew how to walk around an issue and consider it from all angles, the way one might view a sculpture. I valued his advice and often asked him to have a look at things I'd written. He'd invariably give it back to me, saying, "This is great, Alan—I just made a few suggestions." I'd glance through it and find that every sentence was marked up. I didn't mind. Everything I wrote became better for his suggestions. The best writing advice he ever gave me is to assume that my audience is a reasonably intelligent 14-year-old. If you can explain it to that person, anyone can understand it. For Bayless, the point of writing—of all communication—was not to impress, but to connect.

By now, I'm sure you've gathered that for much of my life I thrived on action and accomplishment. I prided myself on my ability to make things happen. My misplaced disappointment in Lee, with what I perceived as his shortfall, was the biggest wedge in our relationship. And it was a wedge of my own creation. At age 87, I now know better, and I'm still learning. One of my "teachers" is Evelyn Johnson, who has a deft way of dislodging my assumptions with her questions and observations.

"In education, we hear a lot about the achievement gap," Evelyn said. "But many scholars in the field are reframing the conversation away from *achievement* to *opportunity* gap."

The term "achievement gap" refers to the chronic and persistent gap in performance of students from marginalized populations—including Latino/Hispanic, Black, and Native Americans, and students with disabilities—when compared with the norm. In our national conversations about education, the default frame of reference ("the norm") is usually a privileged one: White and middle class.

When we use the term "achievement gap," Evelyn explained, it tends to pin the failure on the individual, or on groups of individuals, rather than on environmental or systemic factors. In other words, the phrase blames students for failing to achieve, rather than putting the responsibility on us as a nation for failing to support *all* students and giving them what they need to succeed. Consider the pandemic of 2020. Most students fell behind in learning—not because they were slacking off, but because it took several months for teachers and administrators to figure out how to provide schooling safely in a radically different environment. The "summer slide" in learning that teachers observe in kids every year when they return to school in fall stretched to more than six months in 2020. Suddenly, we were faced with a serious gap in learning that impacted *all* students—a gap of access rather than achievement, clearly the result of a catastrophic environmental event. It was a stark reminder that students from marginalized populations face systemic obstacles in their access to quality education on an ongoing basis. In our county, for example, only 40 percent of all kindergarten students entered schools in 2018 with the reading readiness skills they needed to be successful. For students from low socioeconomic status backgrounds and for Latino/Hispanic students, the percentages were even lower—16 percent and 15 percent, respectively. And during the pandemic, these children fell even further behind their more privileged peers.

"Putting the focus on opportunity rather than achievement," Evelyn said, "makes it a more realistic conversation. Because then we can think long-term and strategically about how we can meet the needs of all children."

Ideally, this would lead us to rethink how public education is funded in our country. The funding of school districts through property taxes bakes in disadvantages for schools in less affluent areas. Underfunded districts have a hard time recruiting and retaining high-quality teachers, and they often lack the budgets for learning-rich programs or even the books and technology their students need.

While Lee Pesky Learning Center doesn't have the power to solve this problem, we can do our part by raising awareness. By partnering with state agencies, universities, and foundations to provide support to some of the most at-risk school districts in Idaho, LPLC is helping to lift the tide for young learners. LPLC also has the agility to formulate and test small-scale, targeted solutions. In the spring of 2020, they quickly pulled together a pilot program to help the children most negatively impacted by the pandemic in Blaine County, the community where Wendy and I happen to live.[51] *Pathways to Literacy*, in partnership with the Community Library, provided for a summer program of eight weeks of one-on-one, free tutoring for a group of first-grade students who are English learners, with ongoing support through the school year. Sessions were held out-doors, and everyone wore masks. The parents of the students were encouraged to work with their children using materials in English and Spanish designed for at-home learning, specially prepared by Lee Pesky Learning Center.

In just one year, due to the need for and success of this program, we were able to garner the necessary funds and community support to double the program for the 2021–22 school year and add an important new element: LPLC is working to hire only Spanish-speaking tutors for Pathways, and it will offer a stipend to offset college costs in an effort to attract potential teachers who are Latino/Hispanic. This program aligns with several of LPLC's strategic commitments, including closing the opportunity gap, preparing the next generation of practitioners, and advancing the research in the science of learning.

Pathways was a just small step in our community, but it made a big difference for the children and their families. Even better, we hope it can serve as a model for communities across our country. We aren't content to shrug and say, "It is what it is"—an expression I detest. If something is worth doing, then let's find a way to make it happen.

I LOVE MY conversations with Evelyn, particularly when they veer to the philosophical. Even then, they usually relate to the work she and her colleagues do at Lee Pesky Learning Center. For example, what it means to be *disabled*. Was Lee disabled? We didn't view or treat him that way, though we knew he struggled with things we couldn't help him with. Is a person with a disability "disabled" in all contexts? Or is disability a function of the environment? For me, this is a provocative and illuminating question.

To be disabled, according to Merriam-Webster, is to be "impaired or limited by a physical, mental, cognitive, or developmental condition."

"But what if you *weren't* impaired or limited in what you could do or accomplish?" Evelyn asked. "What if the environment was suited to your particular challenges, and you could function optimally—as well as people without those challenges—would you still be considered disabled?"

Some specialists make the case that dyslexia shouldn't be called a *learning* disability—it should be called a *print* disability. It's not that people with dyslexia can't learn—on the contrary, they can learn very well in many contexts. What it comes down to is a mismatch between how they process information and the expectations of an environment that places a heavy emphasis on the use of printed materials. Often, if you provide someone with dyslexia access to the information in a different way—via audio, for example—they can comprehend and process the information. The widespread availability of audiobooks and podcasts has made "reading" a lot easier for people with dyslexia, to say nothing of the visually impaired. And while bibliophile purists might look down on audiobooks as "not *real* reading," why does it matter *how* you learn, *how* you get your news, or *how* you come to appreciate literature?

Traditional school environments rely heavily on instructional approaches that don't work for all learners. Moreover, judgments of "success" and "failure" are based on specific markers (i.e., grades and test scores) and on rigid timelines that don't work for kids who have learning issues. Teachers teach to the markers, and parents want their kids to strive to the markers. This is not to say we should get rid of standards. But they might be more useful if they were treated as benchmarks or signposts rather than as finish lines. Goals, based on the recognition that everyone is going to reach them in a different way and at different rates.

Disability can also be a matter of perception, reinforced by the language we use. "There's been extensive research showing that we're shaped by the words we use to describe someone," said Anne Clohessy, LPLC's clinical psychologist. "When we use negative or stigmatizing language to describe someone, we treat them differently—we tend to devalue them."

I think of Muffy Davis as someone who defies stigmatizing categories. She is well known in her hometown of Sun Valley, Idaho, as a gold-winning Paralympian alpine skier and cyclist. She's also a mother, a motivational speaker, and our Idaho state representative. Muffy does not give the slightest impression of being impaired or limited. I have always had full use of my legs, yet I could never have accomplished what Muffy has. Muffy uses a wheelchair. But I wouldn't label her as "handicapped." She is extraordinary.

When I shared these thoughts with Muffy, she pointed out that if you took the definition of disability further, even people who need glasses might be considered disabled. Their adaptive equipment—glasses—helps mitigate visual impairments, much as Muffy's wheelchair and adaptive skis and bike enable her to move and recreate. Muffy has a hard time with labels for the disabled, like "impaired," "handicapped," or "physically challenged." She finds that none of these descriptors really fit her. When she was younger, the term Muffy felt best described her was *physically deviant.* "I know *crazy* and *deviant* generally apply to behavior, but it was the one I liked the best, possibly for shock value. And back then, it was also kind of cool to be considered a deviant!" Refreshing and bold, too, I would add.

At Lee Pesky Learning Center, everyone makes it a point to use language that puts the person first, rather than their perceived deficits. That means taking the time to know and value a person—rather than making quick assumptions and putting them into a category. It's easy to become inured to a particular frame of reference, to view "different" as not normal. There are those who see autism as not normal. ADHD as not normal. Stuttering as not normal. Dyslexia as not normal. Things to be ashamed of. Once upon a time, being left-handed was stigmatized. Left-handers were believed to have dealings with witchcraft or the devil. Seems crazy, doesn't it?

But let's be honest: Many of us feel uncomfortable around people who are different from us—for me, it may be a kid who is heavily pierced and tattooed; for others, it might be someone of a different religion, ethnicity, or sexual orientation. Or a person who uses a wheelchair. We may not know how to act, what to say, or where to look. We may feel unsure of ourselves, embarrassed, even threatened.

For the most part, I believe I embrace diversity and am accepting of people who are different from me. But with Lee, at times, it was another matter. Lee stood out in our family in some ways that made me uncomfortable—because I didn't understand the nature of his differences and I couldn't control them. As his father, I felt protective of him. I was concerned that qualities I perceived as weaknesses might cause him pain and lead to difficulties for him. Also, I worried that they might reflect on me as a father. I was out of my depth because I didn't understand this person I loved, and I didn't know enough at the time to challenge my assumptions.

Understanding and accepting differences are hard. Suspending judgment and putting aside my biases have, at times, required a physical effort on my part. A dismantling of expectations and goals *I thought* I knew to be right and good. And it was Lee who triggered much of that self-reflection and learning for me. Coming to see the differences Lee and I had in a new light has not always been easy. But it has expanded and softened me. And I am the better for it.

Today, our understanding of the brain, with its glorious spectrum of possibilities, shows us (and me) that differences *are the norm*. A diversity of strengths and talents is something to be celebrated. One of my grandchildren was tested for possible reading challenges. After the evaluation was completed, the specialist told me something to the effect, "Your grandkid is more likely to design a great bridge than write a book." This is not to say that a person with dyslexia cannot be an author or journalist. Her point, I believe, was to steer me away from placing too much weight on something that might be difficult for my grandchild, and to highlight his strength in another area—in this case, spatial thinking.

The terms *learning differences*, *learning challenges*, and *learning disabilities* are often used interchangeably now. Many educators and practitioners prefer "differences," because learning occurs on a broad spectrum, and no two people learn in the same way. Yet in our educational system, a designation of "disability" is often needed to qualify for support services mandated by law. These protections are important because our educational system is *not* designed to accommodate all kinds of learners.

Getting back to Evelyn's question, what if you were *not* impaired or limited in what you could learn—for example, because you had found a way to work around your dyslexia, or because the school you attend accommodates many different learning styles? Would you still be considered learning disabled?

I first heard about "universal design" as it relates to education from Evelyn. It's better known in the context of architecture. The term was coined by the architect Ronald Mace working with a group of architects, product designers, engineers, and environmental design researchers at North Carolina State University in the 1990s.[52] Their idea was that buildings and public spaces should be conceived and designed in such a way that they can be easily accessed, enjoyed, and used to the fullest extent possible by all people—regardless of their age, size, or abilities.[53] The Nezu Museum in Tokyo, for example, underwent extensive renovations in 2006 that incorporated barrier-free design elements. Ramps were added, uneven garden pavers were replaced with smooth surfaces, and exhibits were spaced so as to allow easy access for everyone. Artwork and exhibit cases were adjusted to an eye-level height comfortable for elementary school students as well as people seated in wheelchairs.[54] Also called *design for all*, these principles go beyond accessibility for the disabled. They are meant to create spaces that are as welcoming for children as they are for parents with strollers, people in wheelchairs, and the elderly—in recognition that our needs change as we move through life.

Inclusive environments are arguably better for everyone. Chris Downey is an architect who survived a brain tumor. The surgery to remove his tumor was successful, but it resulted in the loss of his sight. In his interview with Lesley Stahl on *60 Minutes*, Downey remarked that he's a better architect unsighted than he was with sight.[55] In learning to rely on his other senses, he has experienced cities, buildings, and spaces in a more holistic and revealing way, becoming aware of things he took for granted when he was sighted. Now he *feels* spaces and *hears* buildings. In his TED talk, Chris jokes, "There are two types of people in the world—those with disabilities, and those who haven't quite found theirs yet." If cities were "designed with the blind in mind," he says, public spaces would be more balanced and generous. Cities would be more just, equitable, and inclusive, benefiting us all.[56]

The principles of universal design have been making inroads in education as well, thanks in large part to CAST—a nonprofit education research and development organization in Massachusetts that created the Universal Design for Learning (UDL) framework, with guidelines being used around the world to make learning more inclusive.[57] Understood.org, one of the most comprehensive and highly regarded resources for those who learn and think differently, describes UDL as a way of thinking about teaching and learning that helps give all students an equal opportunity to succeed.[58] It's encouraging to see so many resources with the latest evidence-based information on learning being made available to parents, students, and teachers.

The term "universal" can be misleading. To be clear, UDL is *not* about finding one approach that works for every child. That doesn't exist. Rather, UDL entails having a variety of teaching methods available to accommodate different learners, while incorporating flexibility in the way students can access and engage with materials. UDL doesn't specifically target kids with learning challenges, but it can be especially helpful for them (even when they haven't been diagnosed), as well as for students learning English.[59]

Even if all classrooms used science-based reading instruction, kids with the most severe learning disabilities would still need remediation. But adopting science-based practices can greatly reduce the number of students overall who need extra help in reading. One in five people has some form of learning disability. This includes students with mild learning challenges who would be well served in classrooms where teachers use these methods. "If we can catch most of the kids who struggle when they're young and help get them off to a strong start learning to read using evidence-based practices," Evelyn said, "then the number of students for whom we would have to provide highly specialized intensive intervention would be so much smaller." Imagine the boost to literacy such an educational approach would provide.

I'm not aware of top-to-bottom UDL schools, but a growing number of schools, colleges, and universities have been moving to incorporate UDL principles into their programs. It's encouraging to see the progress we have made in improving physical access in our public spaces so they can be used more fully by people of different abilities. Thanks to the Americans with Disabilities Act, we're accustomed to seeing elements of more inclusive physical access all around us: wheelchair ramps, automatic doors, Braille signage on elevators, audible pedestrian crossing signals, closed-captioned broadcasts. Why not universal design for education, too?

Universal design for learning sounds idealistic, but it's not far-fetched. In their work to address students' learning needs, LPLC education specialists search for technology-driven solutions that allow students to access information in a variety of ways—which is also an important element of the UDL approach. And the science-based early childhood reading instruction Lee Pesky Learning Center has been promoting throughout Idaho incorporates UDL principles—namely, to help teachers create a context that will be supportive of different learners so that a student with learning disabilities, regardless of where they are on the continuum, will have access to learning in the general education classroom.

Businesses, foundations, and state legislatures have taken note because the results of evidence-based instruction are compelling. As these models become more widely used, as teacher education is adjusted to incorporate science-based instruction as a core curriculum element in all colleges of education, as quality early childhood public education is made available to all families, I believe we will look back and wonder, *What took us so long?*

THE IDEA OF reengineering entire environments and systems to become more inclusive and benefit more learners may be daunting, but it is absolutely worth pursuing. We can also effect change by helping kids to better navigate their *internal* landscapes. An approach formulated by Evelyn in collaboration with the psychologists, reading specialists, and counselors at LPLC is designed to do just that. They refer to it as TPW, or The Pesky Way.

I'll be honest—I don't like the name.

"Why do we have to use that name?" I asked Evelyn.

"That's how we referred to it as we were developing it," Evelyn responded, "and the name just kind of stuck. Can you think of a better one?"

I couldn't.

"That's what I thought," she said. "'The Pesky Way' has traction, so we're sticking with it." Case closed.

TPW is founded on the truth that everyone is a learner—not only students, but teachers, education specialists, and researchers, as well.

Being a learner means being willing to make mistakes. It means adjusting our views, approaches, and methodologies as we get new facts and information. Through self-reflection and change, we find new ways to make things better. And I believe there is no more powerful model for children than to work with teachers and other adults who see themselves as learners too, always evolving and willing to self-correct.

TPW is both a methodology and a mindset. And—here is the key—it applies to *just about everything LPLC does*: one-on-one remediation for kids with learning differences, training teachers in science-based reading instruction, and even the team training LPLC staff members do among themselves. The Pesky Way has come to infuse every layer of the organization and all interactions team members have, both inside and outside the organization. Though the approach bears the name of our family, I had nothing to do with developing it. Here's how I would summarize its essence in layman's terms: LPLC specialists deliver science-based practices so they can be adapted for each person, allowing everyone to "own" their unique pathway to learning or teaching. It's a partnership approach that requires asking questions, listening, and valuing the whole person. As such, all participants in this process of discovery are learners. Coaches and specialists must come to know the student or teacher in order to help them; students and teachers must practice the evidence-based tools recommended by the specialist and find the combination that works best for them. Everyone, no matter what their role, is, in the end, a student—including the specialists at LPLC. This is how we empower people to walk away with adaptable learning skills that can be used beyond the intervention setting or classroom.

First, let's look at how TPW is applied in our work with individual children with learning differences. We begin by gaining an understanding of the child's learning profile. As one might expect, this includes an assessment of their academic skills—reading, writing, math. What they're good at, and what they struggle with. In building a profile, evaluators also look at how the child processes information, and how their social, emotional, behavioral functioning and their family dynamic impact their learning.

This comprehensive evaluation allows LPLC mentors to tailor

evidence-based interventions that are determined by the needs of the whole person, rather than looking only at what's wrong. A 360-degree approach is important because the same learning disability can affect children differently.[60] A student who is dyslexic and has working memory challenges, for example, will need different tools from those of a student who is dyslexic and has a hard time focusing and staying on task.

A critical piece in helping a child build sustainable strategies is *self-regulation*, which has become a bit of a buzzword in the field of education. For us, it means mentoring in a way that helps a child understand their "internal landscape" (my word for it—not a technical term). That is, helping them identify their strengths and challenges and learn how to use behaviors and tools that work best for them. In short, it's about empowering a child, through self-awareness, to harness their strengths so they can become resilient in their learning. Think of it as the difference between *telling* someone how to write a good essay and having them *learn the process* of writing a good essay so they become conversant with and confident using tools like brainstorming, outlining, revising and editing, and summarizing. Self-regulation means learning how to use tools that can help you work through and around obstacles in a variety of learning contexts.

We use TPW with teachers, too. In her professional development work with teachers, Cristianne Lane sees TPW as a means of empowering teachers to move forward from where they are. It's not about indoctrination. No one wants to be talked *at*. Or told what to do. (And I'm no exception.) We know that a science-based approach to teaching works, but not every teacher will absorb the tools in the same way or at the same pace. LPLC professional development coaches have to be able to step back from the approach long enough to *see the teacher*. The teachers also have to be able to see that Cristianne and the other LPLC coaches are practicing what they're preaching.

"We need to walk the talk ourselves," Cristianne told me. At the end of each training, she asks the teachers to reflect with questions such as "What did you see *us* do to help build connection? What did we do that helped with your self-awareness, and our awareness of working with you?" The transparency of self-reflection helps build trust.

For Cristianne, it's exciting to be able to have that conversation with teachers. She and her team work hard to make sure their training is reflective of the greater work LPLC does. "We get together as a group and ask ourselves how we can provide more connection and encourage more interaction," Cristianne explained. "How do we ensure that teachers leave our training with the big ideas and takeaways that we intended them to get out of the training?"

Cristianne and Evelyn are trying to cultivate a culture in which teachers are supported and encouraged to continually ask themselves how they can improve student outcomes. "To do that," Evelyn said, "we at LPLC also have to be willing to learn and ask ourselves the same question every day: How can we do better?"

WENDY AND I have been fully committed to Lee Pesky Learning Center since day one, and we made sure it wouldn't fail. But institutional preservation was never our goal.[61] Our mission has always been to make a positive and sustainable difference in the lives of others. And that requires much more than simply keeping the doors open and the lights on. It is the people who choose to work at LPLC who have made it successful.

I am reminded of something Winston Churchill said in the aftermath of WWII, when he was asked how he was able to raise public morale and galvanize the nation with his speeches. He responded by giving credit to the people of Great Britain and the world. It was *they*, he insisted, who had summoned the courage—"the lion heart"—to withstand tyranny. He merely had "the luck to be called upon to give the roar."[62]

My roar, born of grief, was to create a center in the name of the son we lost. But the extraordinary place LPLC is today has more to do with the lion heart of all those who have poured themselves into the work. And, every day, they challenge my thinking and expand my perspective with the questions they ask and the powerful way they approach the mission of overcoming obstacles to learning.

During the short time Lee was with us, I focused a great deal of attention on what I felt was missing, and, as a result, I saw only a small part of the world that was Lee. I viewed Lee through the frame of my expectations. Now I know Lee better because I see and appreciate and cherish *all* that he was.

I believe that Lee Pesky Learning Center has an impact far beyond its footprint because it views people through a wide lens—with empathy and with a belief in their possibilities and all they are capable of. I consider myself one of the greatest beneficiaries of this learning. How lucky I have been to be part of a circle of passionate, dedicated people who continue to ask, "How can *we* do better?"—a question founded on the belief that it is *always* possible.

Chapter 13

Learning from Lee

I'm looking at the large stack of letters on my desk waiting to be signed and mailed. Next to it is a smaller pile with the 150 letters I've gotten through so far. Every fall I write a letter to my friends and acquaintances about Lee Pesky Learning Center. I love telling people about what we do, but I don't love the feeling of my arthritic wrist after I've signed my name a few hundred times and added a personal note for each recipient. Writing the letter doesn't get any easier. A little bit of Lee and a large part of me goes into each thought I put on the page. And over the past 24 years, every letter has been totally different. The sentiment, however, is always the same: Lee Pesky Learning Center is a labor of love.

In early November 1997, nine months after we opened LPLC's doors, I sat down to compose my first annual letter. It was two-and-a-half pages long, and I ended it with well-known lines from the poet Hugh Robert Orr: "They are not dead who live in hearts they leave behind. In those whom they have blessed they live a life again."[63]

I was determined that Lee's life would continue to have meaning, and opening Lee Pesky Learning Center was the first step.

My first letter went to 120 people. Over the next few weeks, most of them responded, and to each one I sent a thank-you note. Today, I send many more letters and thank-you notes. Every gesture of support, every donation we receive, is confirmation that we are not alone in our labor of love. And I can't thank enough all those who have joined us. The letters have become a dialogue with an ever-widening circle of people who believe in what we are doing and have become an important part of our story. They understand. Lee Pesky Learning Center came into being so others could benefit from what we weren't able to do for our son.

Lee left us 25 years ago. It feels like a long time, but it also feels like the blink of an eye. In a few years, he will have been gone longer than the time he had with us. Heidi and Greg are both married and have raised five children between them. Wendy and I have aged in years, but not in our desire to live our lives to the fullest. My understanding of Lee has deepened, but he is the same: his smile is always broad, his blue eyes sparkle, his bald head grows no hair, and his wit is still sharp and dry. This is the Lee I hold close. He is the one Wendy, Heidi, Greg, and I walk beside, arm in arm. The Lee who lived his life with us.

My role at LPLC has changed over time. I've scaled back my day-to-day involvement and stepped to the sidelines so other more capable and energetic minds can guide the organization and take it into the future. I have loved watching the organization grow and evolve into something I could never have foreseen nor created on my own. My passion for what we do in Lee's name has not diminished, and my commitment is unchanged. Yet, like a parent who has nurtured and guided a child, there comes a time when you have to get out of the way and let it become what it will be.

Still, as long as I breathe, I will be LPLC's biggest cheerleader and most ardent supporter. What could be more fulfilling than changing lives for the better? What could be more important than nurturing an organization that helps children find a pathway to learning that will give them a better chance of fulfilling their potential? My attachment to LPLC has everything to do with children. But mostly, it's about one child in particular.

Lee Pesky Learning Center is personal. It's emotional, raw. If I had allowed it to wither or to be absorbed by a larger institution, it would have been like walking away from the bond I created with Lee after he was gone. Like losing the relationship I wasn't able to have with my son when he was with us. When Wendy is asked what the Center means to her, she says, "Every child who comes to Lee Pesky Learning Center leaves with a little bit of Lee in them." This is also true for me, but there is something else, too: Lee Pesky Learning Center has helped me understand myself and Lee better, and I cherish Lee more for it every day.

This morning while I was working on the letters, an acquaintance stopped by my office to chat. He's a family counselor and mediator, and he wanted to tell me about a couple who had come to him for help.

"Their kid is difficult," he said. "Why isn't he doing better in school, and why is he always so angry? They're really struggling with how to bring him in line. Do you think Lee Pesky Learning Center can help?"

As I listened, two Alans inside me were dueling to respond. One, the father I once was, who always knew best, would have commiserated with parents frustrated by a recalcitrant child. The other Alan, the one I have become, wanted to jump up and shout, "They don't need to bring their son in line with them. He's not the problem. *They* need to understand *him* and the challenges he's experiencing, whatever they may be. They need to get the right help for him. And for themselves."

I hear this again and again from distraught parents: *What do we do? We don't understand. We are at our wit's end.*

But I don't jump up and shout. Instead, I take a breath. Because it took me a while to understand, too.

Let me tell you about Lee.

Acknowledgments

Writing this book has been the biggest adventure of my life. As soon as I took the first step, memories that had been lost for years came back to me. Some I had forgotten. Others, I chose to forget or erase from my mind. It wasn't just remembering, but *understanding* that made this journey different from anything I'd ever experienced. *More to Life than More* became a reflection on how my life changed as a result of the loss of Lee and the creation of Lee Pesky Learning Center. When Wendy and I founded Lee Pesky Learning Center 25 years ago, the possibility that I might become one of its greatest beneficiaries in learning, or that LPLC would one day be recognized as one of the leading facilities of its kind in our country, never entered my mind. Yet that is what has happened. It is also why I decided to write this book.

Thanks to the many caring, passionate people over the years who have made LPLC what it is, I have come to understand what Lee had to contend with in dealing with his learning disabilities. They have given me a deep appreciation and respect for all those who, like Lee, learn differently. Most of all, I've learned that it's not a parent's vision of what they want their child to be that matters. Rather, it is the determination, discipline, and courage children summon in overcoming obstacles to learning that we should celebrate.

Teaching and learning are most effective when we do so as a community, and LPLC is a testament to that. I am deeply grateful to the spectacular staff and board members who have made it possible for LPLC to carry out its mission. Out of all the remarkable people who have played a role in the Center's evolution, two, in particular, must be mentioned: Blossom Turk, who helped me get LPLC started as our founding executive director; and Evelyn Johnson, who is leading LPLC into the future. What I have learned from them could easily fill a book. I am grateful to the parents who entrusted us with their children, the teachers and schools who welcomed LPLC into their classrooms, and the institutions with whom we have collaborated and broken new ground in the science of learning. Most notably, Boise State University's College of Education, Lafayette College, Yale University, and the Sorenson Impact Center at the University of Utah. And with their goodwill and donations, our supporters have been steadfast partners in helping us find pathways to learning for thousands of children. From the very beginning, our goal was to help as many children as possible, irrespective of the financial resources available to their families. The generosity of supporters enables us to serve nearly all those who seek our assistance at the Center and to reach children in far-flung rural communities via distance-learning capabilities. More recently, LPLC was able to launch a program that will help narrow the opportunity gap in learning for children in our immigrant communities who are English-language learners—this too, thanks to our community of donors.

When I decided to write a book, I was aware that I couldn't do it alone. My life was filled with various community and philanthropic involvements, especially my commitment to Lee Pesky Learning Center, which will always be a significant part of my life. Having the desire and energy was not enough. I needed someone to work with whom I could trust. I started at the top, interviewing highly qualified writers with lots of experience, and quickly realized that my book would be just another line on their résumé. Another job. I needed someone to whom I could express my thoughts without reserve. Someone who would be considerate, not judgmental, and make me feel comfortable about navigating emotional terrain. And then I met Claudia.

After our three years working together, I can't believe how fortunate I have been to have Claudia as my coauthor. While Claudia and I had each done a lot of writing, writing a book would be new for both of us. Yet, something clicked when we first met, and it gave me the confidence that we could pull it off. Looking back, I can honestly say that was a tremendous understatement.

Before one word was written, we spent a lot of time talking. Curious and perceptive, Claudia never stopped asking questions, the answers preserved on the recording device that always sat on the table. She always wanted to know more, to delve deeper. I suggested she speak with some of my family members, friends, colleagues, and associates to get perspectives other than my own, and she proved to be more than an adept interviewer. She became their confidante, and together they explored what makes Alan tick.

A few months into the process, Claudia began putting words on paper. Although she'd never written a book and didn't have a degree in psychology (her degree, as it happens, is in international diplomacy), I found she was superb at both. I've never been to a psychologist, never had counseling or therapy. After three years of Claudia digging into the caverns of my life, I have some idea what it must be like to be psychoanalyzed. Yet unlike psychoanalysis, the results of our often raw and emotional conversations would be shared in a book for all to see. Everything was fair game, and it was more than a little unsettling for me at times. We went back and forth on every passage, every chapter until we got it right. And although the book you have just read is Claudia's first, I can't wait to see what this talented and delightful writer produces in the future. Most of all, her own memoir—the book she always wanted to write but hadn't yet found the courage to take on.

I am deeply grateful to everyone who spoke with Claudia. There isn't anyone who told me they didn't enjoy their conversation with her. We appreciate the time and thoughts shared by Cristianne Lane, Anne Clohessy, Israel Catz, Richard Osguthorpe, Susie Luckey, Julianne Masser, and Marvin Sloves, whose thoughts and words we have shared extensively in these pages. Evelyn Johnson generously shared her insights and expertise with us, and she also reviewed and vetted portions of the book related to Lee Pesky Learning Center and the science of learning. My heartfelt thanks also to Lindy Crawford, Camilla Trinchieri and Stuart Greenspon, Suzanne and Mort Marvin, Debbie and Steve Goddard, Nancy and Terry

Curran, Barry Stone, Henry Wallach, Louisa Moats, Matthew Weatherley-White, Andy Pesky, Hope Worcester, Sam Worcester, Mark Stern, and Crissa.

I would also like to extend my gratitude to Tuck professor John Vogel, who wrote the Lee Pesky Learning Center case study and invited me for fifteen consecutive years to participate in his class when the case was discussed. After John retired, Nan Stone succeeded him and continued to extend the annual invitation for me to speak with Tuck students, an experience I have always treasured.

I applaud all those who have dedicated themselves to advancing the science of learning. Like Lisa Gabel, chair of the neuroscience program at Lafayette College, for her groundbreaking scholarly work on the early detection of dyslexia—findings that have the potential to make our work at Lee Pesky Learning Center easier and more impactful. The sooner learning disabilities are identified, the better for the child and the easier it is for teachers, schools, parents, and learning specialists to help them. I have been an enthusiastic and appreciative supporter of Lisa's work for years.

To Peter Ottowitz, with whom I shared a lifetime of laughs that continues every time we talk or get together, thank you. And for two friends who are no longer with us, Alvin Ehrlich and Ariel Halpern, whose steady compass and integrity and sincerity still guide me, I am forever grateful. Until I met Kiki Keating, I always thought I ran fast. She leaves me far behind when it comes to thinking outside the box. Her energy and enthusiasm have no bounds. Julie Ganz, our Skyhorse Publishing editor, was a pleasure to work with. She could not have been more responsive, always available at a moment's notice. As for my assistant, Ivy Slike, whose job description is to make my life easier, I am convinced there is nothing she can't do, including finding my lost keys.

I wish my parents, Belle and Lou, were here so that I could hug them and thank them for all they did. How happy they would be to see how their two sons turned out, the lives they created with the wonderful women they married, and the families they raised. I couldn't be prouder of my younger (and only) brother, Andy, with whom I have an unparalleled friendship.

I met Wendy in 1960, and we were married nine months later. How incredibly blessed I am to have found a life partner who has brought me so much joy, and with whom I have shared so much. I have loved every one of our moments together. If a legacy can be measured by the values parents instill in their children, then I couldn't wish for more than we have in Heidi and Greg. I am in awe of all you have become and the families you have raised.

And to Lee: I think of you every day. Without you, I would not have found the understanding and fulfillment I have now. In writing this book, I have come to know you and love you in a way I never did before.

—*Alan Pesky*

It has been a joy for me to work with Alan on this book, to get to know him and Lee Pesky Learning Center. Over the last few years I have experienced the power of trusting in possibilities in a way I never did before.

In 1996, Blossom Turk, who would become Alan's partner in getting Lee Pesky Learning Center off the ground and its first director, wrote in a letter to her son, "I'm going to take a chance and fly with this guy, Alan Pesky." This revered and experienced educator, who had been the principal of the largest high school in Idaho for 10 years, decided to cancel her retirement plans to start a learning center in Boise, Idaho. This, after meeting Alan for the first time. Sadly, I never knew Blossom, but I often hear her words in my head. As I do Anne Clohessy's about her early work at Lee Pesky Learning Center: "We were building the plane as we were flying it." Like Blossom, Anne used the flight metaphor.

Alan has that effect on people. A visionary who inspires confidence and trust, Alan thrives on doing improbable things that are entirely worth pursuing, and he invites others to join him on the journey. His enthusiasm and energy are contagious, his sincerity and integrity a given. As some of the people I interviewed shared with me about Alan, and which I discovered firsthand, you find yourself suddenly doing things you never imagined. Being swept into the orbit of his action is exhilarating even if there are moments when you think, *Wait, this is crazy.* (Just ask Wendy, who has often said to her husband, "We are going *where*??") But there you are, and there's nothing else you'd rather be doing because Alan believes in you and he has a plan and you know, somehow, something incredible and good will come of it.

I had written extensively throughout my life in a wide range of professional capacities, but I'd never published anything. Yet in my second meeting with Alan, he was asking me if I'd like to help him write his memoir. He could have hired one of the top freelance writers in the country. Instead, he chose me, a person who at 57 had only recently decided to change careers and be a writer. Who raced home after that meeting to Google "how to write a proposal to help someone write a memoir" and, more important, "how to write a memoir."

I knew Alan slightly for years in the way one comes to know most people in a small town—as a nodding acquaintance at the grocery store, a familiar face at local events. Alan and Wendy seemed to exude a warm and genial presence in our Idaho community. They are well known for their founding of Lee Pesky Learning Center and their generous support of local causes and nonprofit organizations. Good people. Whenever I'd catch Alan's gravelly, New York-accented voice in a crowd, I'd find myself leaning in, delighted to hear the comforting accent of my childhood in my adopted state of Idaho.

Our formal introduction came by way of Jenny Emery-Davidson, director of Sun Valley-Ketchum's highly regarded Community Library. I had asked Jenny if she knew of anyone in town who might need help on a writing project, and Alan's name came up. Little did she or I know what was being set in motion, but I will be forever grateful to her. The most marvelous life experiences, I've found, tend to come about by chance rather than design. Meeting Alan was one of them, and it changed my life. In asking me to help him write about his life, he was entrusting me to be the keeper and teller of his story. Trust requires a suspension of fear and doubt, and in that sense it is an act of courage and generosity. Alan is a generous person who believes in a greater good, focuses on possibilities, is not afraid of obstacles, and sees the potential in people. That is how Lee Pesky Learning Center came about. An organization that has thrived on an ethos of humility, inclusiveness, and trust, LPLC embodies the spirit of its founder.

That spirit was also the foundation of our book collaboration, and it allowed us to challenge and disagree with each other. Some days, our discussions were lively and the disagreements vehement. Yet we never once doubted that we both were there for the same purpose: to tell the story that needed to be shared, and to write it in an honest way. I asked questions, prodded, and poked. Alan talked, I wrote, he edited, we debated, and I rewrote. And then we did it all again. We brainstormed, and we course-corrected, always trusting in the narrative that was emerging. Alan gave me a long list of people to interview, and I had free rein to ask what I wanted. Many of the interview transcripts spurred Alan to go even deeper in his reflections, taking him to places neither of us expected.

In this way, the book became an exploration of Alan's life rather than a recounting of his accomplishments. As a first-time book author, I found it remarkable to witness and be part of this. This self-assured, high-achieving, driven man was willing in his 80s to reflect with vulnerability and brutal honesty about his role in the relationships that had challenged him the most. Some of Alan's revelations as he peeled away layers of memories about Lee were gutting. One, in particular, I will never forget. It took me several minutes just to find my voice again. I doubted that I could ever summon the courage to examine my life the way Alan did. Now, because of Alan, I know I can.

Writing with and about Alan gave me ample opportunity for self-examination. When I was a young student and intent on excelling, how did I view classmates who, like Lee, were struggling to learn? When I was raising my daughter, to what extent was I expecting her to follow *my* script? Throughout my life, how often have I judged those whom I perceived to be less successful than I, or just different? Such were the questions I asked myself, and I found the answers unsettling but well worth pondering.

The gifts and learning opportunities afforded to me during my work on this book have been boundless. Lee Pesky Learning Center team members took me under their collective wing and introduced me to the science of learning. My greatest regret is that I did not have the benefit of their wisdom until I was in my fifties. I am in awe of the work they do every day in helping children find a pathway to learning.

I'm particularly grateful to Evelyn Johnson and Cristianne Lane for their patience and cheerful support of my efforts to capture the scope and essence of LPLC in these pages. And to everyone else who was willing to be interviewed by me, your contributions broadened my perspective and brought a depth and richness to the book that we could not have achieved without you. The marvelous Pesky family welcomed me with open hearts and open arms. As with Alan, the support I received from Wendy, Heidi, and Greg was extraordinary. And Lee, whom I wish I had known, seemed to be ever-present in our conversations and our writing.

Alan and I were blessed to have a superb editor and coach, the delightful and brilliant Sarah Sentilles. She is the award-winning author of *Draw Your Weapons* as well as four other outstanding books, a writing teacher par excellence, and an activist who has made a tremendous difference in Idaho in her work advocating for some of our most vulnerable communities. She was able to coax our best writing out of us by pointing out what we had to let go of, where we needed to go deeper, and when we should let things be messy. We are immensely grateful to Sarah, a writer whose integrity and compassion I will always strive to emulate. My thanks also to Garrard Conley, author of *Boy Erased*, who was my teacher at the esteemed Fine Arts Work Center in Provincetown. His tutelage and insights set me on a true course for my work on this book.

Everyone needs friends who can tell you when you are not being true to yourself and who can switch at a moment's notice from cheerleading to mop-up duty. Sheila Liermann, Jan Peppler, and Margaret Work, this would have been so much harder without your friendship. My gratitude to Cal Millar, who was there when the creative floodgates opened for me (and who was at least partially responsible for flipping the switch); and to Ivy Slike, for not waiting for me to make the call. Tim Silva, mentor and hands-down the best boss ever, recognized and lauded the writer in me and graciously saw me on my way out of a perfect job. And were it not for soul warrior Juliana Jones-Munson, who kicked my butt and never, ever let me weasel out, I would not be a writer.

My husband, Ralph Pavone, never took umbrage when I was too lost in my writing head to hear what he was saying. He always managed to coax me out of a fetal position when the writing got tough and push me out the door for fresh air and hikes. My bonus children, David and Gabrielle, and Hamburg family contingent, Peggy and Christoph, cheered me on. Heike Kubasch, my sister, inspired me with her courage to begin writing long before I did. And Alexandra, my shining light, never wavered in her belief in me. In her good-witchy, buddha-like wisdom, she always knew I could do this.

More to Life than More has allowed me to become a more courageous writer and, I hope, a more thoughtful parent, partner, and friend. Hanging around a person like Alan Pesky can do that.

—*Claudia Aulum*

Endnotes

1   "Timeline of Learning Disabilities," All about learning disabilities and ADHD, LD Online, last modified 2006, http://www.ldonline.org/article/11244/.

2   "5 Historical Figures Who Overcame Learning Disorders," Program Guide, Masters in Special Education, accessed January 13, 2021, https://www.masters-in-special-education.com/lists/5-historical-figures-who-overcame-learning-disorders/.

3   Lloyd Ultan, in collaboration with The Bronx Historical Society, *The Beautiful Bronx, 1920–1950* (New York: Harmony Books, 1979), 11.

4   Ted Morgan, "New! Improved! Advertising!" *New York Times*, January 25, 1976, 248, 258, 259.

5   Lou Gerhig, "Farewell" (speech, Yankee Stadium, New York, July 4, 1939), https://www.lougehrig.com/biography/.

6   Jelani Cobb, "Classnotes: What's Really at Stake When a School Closes," *The New Yorker*, August 1, 2015, https://www.newyorker.com/magazine/2015/08/31/class-notes-annals-of-education-jelani-cobb.

7   "Glioblastoma (GBM)," Tumor Types, American Brain Tumor Association, accessed January 13, 2021, https://www.abta.org/tumor_types/glioblastoma-gbm/.

8   "Glioblastoma Multiforme," Neurosurgical Conditions and Treatments, American Association of Neurological Surgeons, accessed January 13, 2021, https://www.aans.org/Patients/Neurosurgical-Conditions-and-Treatments/Glioblastoma-Multiforme.

9   Ron Fournier, *Love That Boy: What Two Presidents, Eight Road Trips, and My Son Taught Me About a Parent's Expectations.* (New York: Harmony Books, 2016).

10 SE Shaywitz, JM Fletcher, JM Holahan, AE Shneider, KE Marchione, KK Stuebing, DJ Francis, KR Pugh, BA Shaywitz, Persistence of dyslexia: the Connecticut Longitudinal Study at adolescence. Pediatrics. 1999 Dec;104(6):1351–9. doi: 10.1542/peds.104.6.1351. PMID: 10585988. https://pubmed.ncbi.nlm.nih.gov/10585988/.

11 The Connecticut Longitudinal Study also tracks gender composition, neurobiologic basis, and early identification of dyslexia.

12 Marcia D'Arcangelo, "Learning about Learning to Read: A Conversation with Sally Shaywitz," *Educational Leadership*, Volume 57, no. 2 (October 1999): 26–31.

13 Ibid.

14 "The State of Learning Disabilities: Understanding the 1 in 5," Research, National Center for Learning Disabilities (NCLD), 2017, https://www.ncld .org/wp-content/uploads/2017/03/1-in-5-Snapshot.Fin_.03142017.pdf.

15 Ibid.

16 D. Kathryn Currier Moody, "Dyslexia in the Prison Population," *Education Update Online*, December 2008, http://www.educationupdate.com/archives /2008/DEC/html/spec—dyslexia.html#:~:text=While%20the%20prevalence %20of%20dyslexia,Texas%20Department%20of%20Criminal%20 Justice%20.

17 Jay P. Greene, PhD, "The Cost of Remedial Education: How Much Michigan Pays When Students Fail to Learn Basic Skills," Mackinac Center for Public Policy, September 2000, https://www.mackinac.org/S2000-05.

18 Army Maj. Gen. Dennis Laich (ret.), "Commentary: Recruiting's slippery slope," *Army Times*, July 27, 2018, https://www.armytimes.com/opinion/commentary /2018/07/28/recruitings-slippery-slope/: Mark Perry, "The Recruitment Problem The Military Doesn't Want To Talk About," *The American Conservative*, August 15, 2018, https://www.theamericanconservative.com/articles/the -recruitment-problem-the-military-doesnt-want-to-talk-about/.

19 "Gold Key Ceremony Echoes with News of the McCabe Shop," *Advertising Age*, April 19, 1967, 123.

20 Steven Pearlstein, "Reinventing Xerox Corp.," *Washington Post*, June 29, 1998, https://www.washingtonpost.com/archive/politics/1998/06/29/reinventing -xerox-corp/f9ef9410-d8b5-4462-a1e3-8767232227ae/.

21 Alan Brinkley, "The Legacy of John F. Kennedy," *The Atlantic*, August, 2013, https://www.theatlantic.com/magazine/archive/2013/08/the-legacy-of-john -f-kennedy/309499/.

22 "The Fierce, Fabulous Legacy of Mary Wells Lawrence," Timeline-Event, 4A's, accessed January 28, 2021, https://www.aaaa.org/timeline-event/mary-wells -lawrence-fabulous-first-female-advertising-ceo/.

23 Alexis Clark, "When Jim Crow Reigned Amid the Rubble of Nazi Germany," *New York Times Magazine*," February 19, 2020, https://www.nytimes.com /2020/02/19/magazine/blacks-wwii-racism-germany.html.

24 Paula Span, "The Adman Writes Again," *Washington Post*, May 23, 1991, https://www.washingtonpost.com/archive/lifestyle/1991/05/23/the-adman -writes-again/06ebfd07-4ed7-4f50-8416-e5a011cdcef4/?noredirect=on&utm _term=.f14eb054d808;.

25 Morgan, "New!"

26 Joan Didion, "On Being Unchosen by the College of One's Choice," in *Let Me Tell You What I Mean* (New York: Knopf, 2013).

27 Clayton M. Christiansen, "How Will You Measure Your Life?" *Harvard Business Review*, July-August, 2010, https://hbr.org/2010/07/how-will-you-measure -your-life.

28 Christian McAdams, "Frank Perdue is Chicken!" *Esquire*, April 1, 1973, https: //classic.esquire.com/frank-perdue-is-chicken/#!&pid=114.

29 Larry Hampel, "All in the Family," *Scali McCabe Sloves: A Look Back, March 13–April 10, 1996* (New York: The One Show For Art & Copy, 1996), 23.

30 Joy Golden, "'Don't Kiss Me,' Ed Screamed," *Scali McCabe Sloves: A Look Back, March 13–April 10, 1996* (New York: The One Show For Art & Copy, 1996), 20.

31 Tom Nathan, "There Was This Great Big Guy Named McCabe," *Scali McCabe Sloves: A Look Back, March 13–April 10, 1996* (New York: The One Show For Art & Copy, 1996), 27.

32 Earl Carter, "To Face Fear," *Scali McCabe Sloves: A Look Back, March 13–April 10, 1996* (New York: The One Show For Art & Copy, 1996), 24.

33 Bob Schmetterer, "April Fools, Day, 1971," *Scali McCabe Sloves: A Look Back, March 13–April 10, 1996* (New York: The One Show For Art & Copy, 1996), 35.

34 Alan D. Pesky, "Leading From Values," *Leader to Leader/Hesselbein & Company*, published by Wiley Periodicals LLC on behalf of University of Pittsburgh, October 13, 2020, https://onlinelibrary.wiley.com/doi/epdf/10.1002/ltl.20543.

35 "How One Idaho Boy Has Learned To Be Empowered By His Dyslexia," 2020, Gemma Gaudette, Idaho Matters, *Boise State Public Radio*. March 11, 2020, https://www.boisestatepublicradio.org/post/how-one-idaho-boy-has-learned-be-empowered-his-dyslexia#stream/0.

36 Michael Lewis, "Don't Eat Fortune's Cookie" (baccalaureate remarks, as prepared, Princeton University, Princeton, NJ, June 3, 2012), https://www.princeton.edu/news/2012/06/03/princeton-universitys-2012-baccalaureate-remarks.

37 Matthew J. Slaughter and Matthew Rees, "The Slaughter & Rees Report," December 16, 2019, Tuck Center for Business, Government & Society.

38 "Results from the 2019 Mathematic and Reading Assessments," *The Nation's Report Card*, US Department of Education, Institute of Education Sciences, National Center for Education Statistics, National Assessment of Educational Progress (NAEP), various years, 1990–2019, https://nces.ed.gov/nationsreportcard/reading/.

39 Katherine Long, "What, exactly, does science say about reading instruction?" *Seattle Times*, April 5, 2020, https://www.seattletimes.com/education-lab/what-exactly-does-science-say-about-reading-instruction/.

40 Nicholas Kristof, "We're No. 28 And Dropping!" *New York Times*, September 9, 2020, https://www.nytimes.com/2020/09/09/opinion/united-states-social-progress.html.

41 "2020 Social Progress Index—United States," Scorecard, Social Progress Index, accessed January 15, 2021, https://www.socialprogress.org/?tab=2.

42 UNICEF Office of Research (2013), "Child Well-being in Rich Countries: A comparative overview," Innocenti Report Card 11, UNICEF Office of Research, Florence, https://www.unicef-irc.org/publications/pdf/rc11_eng.pdf.

43 "Illiteracy by the Numbers," Literacy Project, accessed January 15, 2021, https://www.literacyprojectfoundation.org/.

44 Amanda Rock, "Universal Pre-K in the United States," Very Well Family, last

updated September 17, 2020, https://www.verywellfamily.com/universal-pre
-k-2764970.

45   Kate Kelly, "What is Decoding?" Trouble with Reading, Understood, accessed
January 15, 2021, https://www.understood.org/en/learning-thinking-differences
/child-learning-disabilities/reading-issues/decoding-what-it-is-and-how-it
-works.

46   "Idaho Early Literacy Project (IELP): Year One Student Growth Results," News,
Lee Pesky Learning Center, September 19, 2019, https://www.lplearningcenter
.org/idaho-early-literacy-project-ielp-year-one-student-growth-results/.

47   The LPLC team trained 100 preschool educators and 100 K–2 teachers in science-based reading instruction. Coaches observed the teachers in their classrooms every month so that they could provide regular feedback through individual coaching with each teacher. Lesson plans, resources, and consistent follow-up
by LPLC were all part of the support provided to teachers in the program. The
reading level for all children was tested when they began the school year, and
again at the end of the school year.

48   "Solving The Special Ed Teacher Shortage: Quality, Not Quantity." 2016,
Scott Simon, Weekend Edition Saturday *Boise State Public Radio*. January 16,
2016. https://www.npr.org/sections/ed/2016/01/16/462181638/solving-the
-special-ed-teacher-shortage-quality-not-quantity.

49   "About PLCs," About, All Things PLCs, accessed January 15, 2020, https:
//www.allthingsplc.info/about.

50   "Obituary of Bayless Manning," Obituaries, Summers Funeral Homes, accessed
January 15, 2021, https://summersfuneral.com/tribute/details/43262/Bayless
-Manning/obituary.html.

51   When I speak about LPLC, I sometimes say, "we," other times, "they." I include
myself in the collective ("we") when it comes to the vision, spirit, and goals of
LPLC, because I still play an active role in this capacity. When I describe the
day-to-day work or management of the organization, which I am not involved
in, I refer to the players as "they."

52   "About the Center: Ronald L. Mace," The Center for Universal Design, NC
State University, accessed January 15, 2021, https://projects.ncsu.edu/ncsu
/design/cud/about_us/usronmace.htm.

53   "The Principles of Universal Design," About UD, The Center for Universal
Design, NC State University, accessed January 15, https://projects.ncsu.edu
/ncsu/design/cud/about_ud/udprinciplestext.htm.

54   Hiroki Endo, "Inclusive Tokyo: Josh's take on barrier-free Nezu Museum," *The Asahi
Shimbun*, February 10, 2020, http://www.asahi.com/ajw/articles/13080459?fb
-clid=IwAR0Lob-Gnsiuyt_0CguuF0fBjPYv9mbXNtmgmNEVBy4mUFlnIIO
-0vJbhoy4.

55   Lesley Stahl, "Architect goes blind, says he's actually gotten better at his job," *60
Minutes*, CBS News, August 11, 2019.

56   Chris Downey, "Design with the blind in mind" (presentation, TEDCity2.0,
October, 2013), https://www.ted.com/talks/chris_downey_design_with_the
_blind_in_mind.

57 "About CAST," Who We Are, CAST, accessed January 15, 2021, https://www
    .cast.org/about/about-cast.
58 Amanda Morin, "What is Universal Design for Learning (UDL)?" Educational
    Strategies, Understood, accessed January 15, 2021, https://www.understood.org
    /en/learning-thinking-differences/treatments-approaches/educational-strategies
    /universal-design-for-learning-what-it-is-and-how-it-works.
59 Ibid.
60 Erin McIntyre, "An individualized approach to training special ed teachers,"
    K-12 DIVE, February 4, 2016, https://www.k12dive.com/news/an-individualized
    -approach-to-training-special-ed-teachers/413180/.
61 Pesky, "Leading."
62 "Churchill the Orator," The Life of Churchill/Man of Words, International
    Churchill Society, accessed January 15, 2021, https://winstonchurchill.org
    /the-life-of-churchill/life/man-of-words/churchill-the-orator/.
63 Hugh Robert Orr, "They Softly Walk," https://uuwestport.org/they-softly-walk/.